Waking Up Alone

Grief & Healing

by
Julie K. Cicero, MSW

Bloomington, IN Milton Keynes, UK

authorHOUSE™

AuthorHouse™
1663 Liberty Drive, Suite 200
Bloomington, IN 47403
www.authorhouse.com
Phone: 1-800-839-8640

First published by AuthorHouse 12/26/2007

ISBN: 978-1-4259-9763-2 (sc)

Library of Congress Control Number: 2007901901

Printed in the United States of America
Bloomington, Indiana

This book is printed on acid-free paper.

I dedicate this book to my sons
Mike and Nick
&
To my hospice colleagues
Our patients and their families

Contents

Acknowledgements

Writing this book was a pleasure as well as a healing process. However, I would be remiss in failing to mention all of my friends and family members who encouraged this writing as well as those who were willing to read and edit. Their contributions were necessary and meaningful. For this, I am forever grateful to Chris, Tina, Mary, Helen, Carol, Doug, Barb and Suzanne.

I would also like to acknowledge and thank all of the people who helped Mike, Nick and I survive Joe's sudden death. They include, but are probably not limited to Joe's friends & "family" from Fort Lee, Allegheny and law school, our friends at St. Patrick's School & Church, in Tacoma, Washington, David Hovland, MSW, our friends and neighbors, co-workers at Reliance and Mutual of Enumclaw, and most notably our immediate (adult) family members, who include Anne, Don, Lois, Terri, Blaine, Kyle, Allison, Mary, John, Lori, Frankie & Lee.

A special thanks to Myrth Ogilvie, MSW, PhD, whose encouragement & instruction was beyond measure, the faculty and staff at the University of Washington/Tacoma Department of Social Work for a meaningful educational experience and finally the Tacoma Youth Symphony for providing the background music for much of this work.

I am forever grateful to my husband, Chris for allowing us to honor and remember Joe, on a sometimes-daily basis and for listening, editing and supporting me in this project and a special thank you to Chuck and Tina for including me in their family circle. Most significantly, I would like to thank my late husband, Joe, for Mike and Nick the absolute joys of my life.

*"The most I ever did for you
was to out live you.
But that is much"*

Edna St. Vincent Millay

Introduction

On January 31, 2001, my husband died while riding snowmobiles with friends in the Cascade Mountains of Washington State. Our sons were only seven and four. His sudden death propelled us into a state of grief, confusion and shock. We soon began counseling and struggled daily with our attempt to assimilate our profound loss. Our new life was one we barely recognized and certainly never would have chosen.

At some point in the early months, Angela (a mother from the boy's school) suggested we meet for coffee at her house. Her first husband had died many years before and she wanted me to meet the woman who had helped her through that difficult time. Within a week, we had six people included in our informal get together. We continued to meet for several months and as others joined in, it was clear that regardless of our circumstances, we benefited from each other's support.

Then during a session with the boy's grief counselor, I envisioned an opportunity for a new career. In observing David's interactions with Mike and Nick, I considered the possibility of working with people who were grieving because of a death. I learned that a master's degree in social work was required in order to work with this population in a profession capacity. Fortunately, a local university offered an MSW program and accepted my application. While in school, and with some tentativeness, I interned at a local hospice agency and immediately recognized that I had found a new path for the second half of my career life.

Waking up Alone contains an in-depth focus on the death of a companion, a compilation of information, reflecting my personal journeys as well as my professional experiences in hospice work – work that includes daily interactions with people who are watching their spouses die as well as work with widows through grief education and support groups.

I frequently use the words widow and spouse and yet the focus is on couples, regardless of marital status. Unfortunately, it is too distracting to say widow-widower-spouse-significant other-partner-girlfriend-boyfriend, in each reference, so throughout the book I interchange the words spouse and companion in representation of all relationships.

Because of my personal and a majority of my professional experience, I focused on the death of a companion as opposed to grief associated with losing a parent, sibling or child. Granted there are similarities in the grief associated with these other losses, however, there are also differences and I chose not to branch out, because the death of a spouse is what I know best.

Since most couples do not die simultaneously, it makes sense that all relationships, which do not end in divorce, end with one partner outliving the other. However, even if we know that our spouse is dying, I do not believe that we can ever be totally prepared. As with all major life events, many adjustments are required.

According to the Census Bureau, approximately 2.5 million Americans over the age of 25 died in 2004 and an estimated 55% indicated married or couple status. This means that nearly 1.3 million people lose their companions annually. As in my case, many of these individuals are young, in their 30s, 40s and 50s– when they suffer this devastating loss. Remarkably, there are few books addressing this issue.

In *Waking up Alone,* I present the multilayered experiences that surround a spouse's death. It is necessary and important to distinguish between sudden and anticipated deaths because they are a different experience. It is equally important to identify the complex aspects of the resultant grief, addressing both the death (the primary loss) and what the death means to you (the secondary losses).

A common thread throughout this book is an examination of our cultural disconnect in America with matters of death and dying. This aversion - or at times outright denial - becomes apparent to us rather immediately as our spouses wrestle with a life ending disease or following their sudden death. The inability of friends and family to deal with death and dying is confusing and hurtful and at times can interfere with our healing process.

My current work at hospice allows me the opportunity to interact with people who are struggling with comprehending the unfamiliar path their lives have taken, while simultaneously seeking validation of their feelings. As the shock subsides and the healing begins, it is crucial for survivors to identify and understand their own emotions and reactions as well as the actions and reactions of friends and family.

If you are reading this book because you have suffered the death of your companion, then you have my heartfelt sympathy. I firmly believe that in order to heal we must understand why we feel the way we do and it is helpful to learn that we are not alone. In your search for even ground, I am hopeful that you will find some constructive information as well as a measure of comfort, compassion and healing within the pages of this book.

*"The world became
eternally divided into
a before and after."*

Tove Ditlevsen

The Sudden Death of a Spouse

Every family is comprised of many stories, which in their telling establish the oral history particular to that family. Sudden death affects the family so intensely, so emotionally, that the story captivates, connecting generations and leaving the survivors to speculate as to how life would have been different, if only...

Our Story

January 31st, 2001, began strangely because I awoke with a chilling premonition, a peculiar awareness that this was not going to be a good day. The focus of this concern was my husband, Joe, who was sleeping soundly at that moment. I looked at him and considered the possibilities. Knowing that he planned to go snowmobile riding in the Cascade Mountains generated an internal alarm. He had only ridden snowmobiles on a handful of occasions; however, to his credit, he was athletic, coordinated and seemingly immortal.

For the next 120 seconds, my mind surfed the possibilities and quickly identified the most likely and definitely the most devastating outcome. I gave thought to him crashing his snowmobile into a tree and considered the prospect of his dying as a result. This thought process undoubtedly sounds somewhat detached, and it was, because during this contemplation, I never truly believed that this scenario would come to fruition.

Even so, I transitioned to the next level and considered what I would do if he actually died. Since I could not have possibly envisioned the fallout from his death, my thinking was totally void of emotion. Instead,

I made a mental checklist of whom I would call and what items I would need to accomplish, and in what order.

At about the time I finished this fatalistic line of thinking, Joe's alarm sounded. As he rolled over, I looked at him straight on and said, "Be careful out there today and don't hit any trees." He responded with a throaty laugh and rolled out of bed. He sometimes suggested that I was too careful, bordering on uptight, and that I needed to relax a little.

Recreational risk taking was not included in my genetic makeup; however, occasional fatalistic thinking was. Fortunately, my worst-case scenarios rarely coincided with reality. That aside, I was unable to elude the ominous sensations that had penetrated my consciousness on this morning.

Our sons, Nick and Mike, were four and seven years old. We roused them from their slumber and shortly thereafter, the day began in earnest. An hour later, I stood in front of the bathroom mirror applying makeup, while the boys splashed and laughed in the bathtub. Joe strolled into the room, elated that his destination was the mountains and not the office. He kissed me goodbye, patted his son's heads, said "Ciao", and ran down the stairs, and out the front door.

We never saw him again.

Customarily Joe drove the kids to school because I had to leave early for work. Since he was unavailable that day, the task was mine, and after much cajoling, I loaded them both in the family van and with their lunch sacks and backpacks in tow, we left for school.

Much to Joe's chagrin and for some unknown reason, I had developed a bad habit of closing the sliding door of the van by using the interior handle. I would reach inside the door and pull on the inside handle always before having managed to get my hand out of the way before it closed.

However as the omens of the morning had hinted, we arrived at school and while the kids waited impatiently on the sidewalk, I failed to pull my hand out of the door in time. A ring on my right hand caught inside the doorjamb. When the door slammed shut, it drove the top edge of the ring deep into my knuckle.

The wave of nausea and stab of pain were instantaneous. Mike, our oldest, surveyed the situation, shrugged it off and took off up the hill to meet his friends. As I fought down the bile (my body's primary reaction to injury), Nick grabbed my other hand, somehow recognizing that I needed human connection at that moment.

We entered the school's office where I asked for ice. Blood oozed from my rapidly swelling knuckle, swelling that was trapping the ring solidly in place. Karma, the secretary (not the metaphysical destiny) surveyed the situation and suggested someone else escort Nick to his class. However, he steadfastly refused her offer and clutched tightly to my other hand.

As she administered some basic first aid, I shared with her my imaginings of the morning. I told her that I knew something bad was going to happen today. Then with a shrug, as though to clear the morning's cobwebs, I added, "But I thought it was going to happen to Joe, not to me."

Karma, having provided me with a bag of ice and a band-aid, looked on quizzically without issuing a comment, (though I am not sure what she could have said) and Nick and I left for his classroom. We must have been quite a sight, as we walked through the crowded hallways with Nick holding my left hand, tears streaking down my face and blood trickling down the wrist of my right hand, which was clutching the ice.

I caught sight of my friend Mary among the many excited preschool children and their parents. She stopped me and offered help, quickly adding that she was already late for a field trip so there was not much she could do at that moment. I assured her that I could drive myself and that I would survive my injuries.

Nick finally released my hand, said goodbye and trudged into his classroom. I managed my way back to the car and drove to my mother's house a few miles away. I undoubtedly caused her concern and caught her totally off guard, barreling through the front door, sobbing and holding my hand out as if it was a foreign object. Once she understood the cause of my dramatic entrance, she drove me straight to the hospital.

The emergency room staff cut off the ring, took x-rays, administered a tetanus shot, sewed eight stitches into the knuckle and applied a splint. Five hours later, they sent me out the door with a prescription for Vicodin.

After picking up the prescription, I was back at home, trying to relax on the living room couch. Unfortunately, the throbbing in my hand, coupled with the adrenaline rush of the day, interfered with any hope I had for a quick nap before the kids arrived home from school.

Then the phone calls started. Concerned friends were checking on me and I was calling everyone else to share with them my premonition and the resultant drama of the day. I kept saying how surprised I was that the "bad thing" I had envisioned that morning had happened to me and not to Joe. At some point, the Vicodin kicked in and dulled the pain, as the narcotic-induced cobwebs took hold, clouding my thoughts.

At around 2:00 p.m., I reached Tanya, the wife of one of the snow-mobile riders. I inquired about their location and estimated arrival time back home. I assured her that I was okay and that there was no need for a quicker return, though she might let Joe know that I would probably not be very helpful that night with the kids. (Had he returned home, he would have easily picked up the slack, cooked dinner, put the kids to bed, and probably would have taken the opportunity to tell me that maybe now was a good time to find a different way to shut the van door). As it was, Tanya called back a few minutes later and advised that the men were on their way back down the trail. It was not clear when they would get home, but at least they were on their way.

Several days later Joe's friends shared with me that he had tried calling home from the ridge top after hearing about my experience, but the line was busy. I often wondered what we would have said and if anything would have made a difference in the outcome of that day. At some point, I realized that no matter how many times I replayed the day's events, I was powerless to turn back the clock.

Eventually, mom arrived with the boys and their backpacks, back from school. Mike brought home his friend Evan who reported that his mom, Mary, would retrieve him on her way home from work. Mom left after she determined that all was well and that Joe's arrival was on the horizon. An hour later, Mary swooped in, picked up Evan, and in comedic sympathetic fashion dropped off a can of Campbell's instant soup. She said I should call her if I needed anything further.

Nick collapsed on the couch, out for his afternoon nap. Mike plunked down on the living room floor alternating between his second grade math assignment and a variety of mindless cartoons, with greater focus on the television.

Then the telephone call came.

> *Anyone who has learned about the death of a spouse by telephone, experiences an overwhelmingly visceral response when recalling that phone call. A memory indelibly imprinted in one's brain, delineating every nuance of the conversation, a conversation that we replay thousands of times over in a feeble attempt to wrap our minds around the message.*

My telephone call came at 5:00 p.m. It was dark outside and January cold. I felt chilled, but unable to distinguish if it was from my injury, the Vicodin or the draft wafting through our 70-year-old house. Tanya's husband, Brian was on the other end of the phone.

Initially, he asked for my mother, an extremely unusual request, compounded by the oddness of his calling in the first place. My mind attempted to work through the confusion, a process complicated by the effects of the medication. I recall that my breathing instantly became heavier and more erratic as I informed him that mom had gone home. He stammered, his voice jumped an octave and then he asked for her home phone number, and I knew. I knew in my mind, my heart and my soul.

Because I didn't answer, he paused only for a second, and then he said, "There's been an accident, Joe's dead." That was all he said - an amazingly few number of words for such a profoundly horrible message.

I could hear my heart beat in my ears, pounding, dizzying. My eyes darted from Mike to Nick, from couch to floor. Our life as we knew it had just ended and I was in a full-blown state of panic.

Later, I reflected that it felt like we lived in one of those decorative snow globes that you see at Christmas and that some unkind hand had picked up our globe, shaken it violently, and then as if to make a cruel point, left us upside down. Regardless of my attempts, I could not catch my breath. Our world was spinning in semi-slow motion and it was all terribly surreal. It felt as though time in our house, in our world, had jumped the track and we were floating off into space.

I picked up the telephone and called my mom because it was the only number I could remember. Her line was busy. My most significant memory of those initial moments was that my eyes kept darting frantically from Mike to Nick to the phone. It was as if my eye movements and my breathing were in a state of hyper-speed, while the rest of me remained frozen to the chair.

At some point, I asked Mike to find me a phone book. (I didn't believe that my legs would support me if I tried to walk). He asked me which book I wanted, the address book or the school directory. I just looked at him, shaking my head, unable to focus on or respond to his question. Eventually he went off on his own and located the address book, eyeing me curiously, as he handed it over.

I found Mary's number, called her, whispered that I needed her to come back. I remember that my voice was thick and shaking as the adrenaline pumped through me. She said she would be right over. Strangely, she never asked why. Maybe she sensed the gravity of the situation or maybe the reason for my request just didn't matter to her.

Nevertheless, I still had to tell her, possibly only to see if I could actually say that Joe was dead. After she hung up the telephone, she reportedly turned to her husband and said, "I think she just told me that Joe is dead." She struggled with comprehending the message, assuming and undoubtedly hoping that she had heard incorrectly.

Mary arrived within minutes and found me sitting at the kitchen table. I asked her to call my mom and then I called Mike into the kitchen. I carefully wrapped my arms around him and then told him that his father had been in an accident. He looked straight at me, eyes wide, scared, his body shaking slightly and asked, "He's all right isn't he?" I said, "No honey, he's dead." Initially, he looked crestfallen, and then he started screaming out the word "No" stretching it out for what seemed like an eternity. All I could do for him was hold on tight.

Nick, awakened by the screams, stumbled into the kitchen, confused and scared. He reached his hand out for me. However, before I could move towards him or say anything, Mike yelled at him, "Nick, dad's dead." Nick stared at us for only a moment, then simply turned around and headed back for the couch, where he had been sleeping peacefully only moments before.

In the interim, Mary had reached my mom and was trying to tell her the news over Mike's screams. Unfortunately, it was all too confusing and chaotic for mom to comprehend what Mary was trying to tell her. After countless repetitions of "Joe's dead," mom eventually heard what Mary was saying, though I do not think she really understood. I soon discovered that no one comprehended this news easily.

At this point, I will try to explain why Joe's death was so hard for everyone to believe. He managed to maintain a constant level of intense energy rivaled by few. A close friend described him as "having spent a great majority of his life with a face consisting of 80% smile and 20% nose" adding that he was "contagious." He was one hundred percent Sicilian, spoke English as a second language and had an almost unparalleled passion for life. He commonly ran into the house yelling for us to come outside with him just in time to catch a spectacular sunset or a collection of shooting stars. He would round a corner and pull off the side of the road because Mt. Rainier looked especially grand at that moment or maybe he spied a hawk flying overhead.

He lived for physical exercise, loved home cooked food and took great care of his family and his friends. He treated everyone equally regardless of his or her position in life. Joe had an uncanny ability to convince whomever he was with that he/she was the most important person in his life and at that moment, it was true.

Joe was a lawyer who missed his calling as a logger, an angler or a dockworker. His fantasy day included hiking in the mountains followed by a beer, a sandwich and a game of pool at the local tavern. He was never comfortable on the inside of any building, so wearing a suit and tie, stuck in a courtroom or in an office all day, was seemingly unnatural for him. Aside from supporting his family and his home, he worked solely so he could afford to play.

So, simply stated, on that cold and wet winter day, when he died so suddenly, it seemed more confusing, more significant, because he seemed so much more alive than the rest of us, and even a little invincible.

I think this quote from Alphonse de Lamarline resonated with the type of person Joe was to everyone who knew him. "There are some people who, when they die, the whole world seems depopulated."

*"One false step
can bring
everlasting grief"*

Chinese Proverb

Understanding Shock

Sudden death occurs because of an undetected and fatal medical condition such as a heart attack or aneurysm and from accidents or acts of violence. Even though some differences exist because of how your spouse died, the common denominator linking the survivors of an unexpected death is shock.

> *When notified that your spouse has died suddenly, the ensuing shock is brutal. It impedes your ability to comprehend news of this magnitude. While you struggle with this attack on your sense of reality, your sense of the world, you cannot possibly anticipate the subsequent physical and emotional impact that it will have on your life.*

I believe that shock is nature's natural intervention, which works as a time- released filter, a filter that allows only fragments of the truth in at any one time. The ultimate purpose of this filter is to regulate both emotional and physical awareness. This filtering is necessary in order for our minds to absorb both the death and its meaning, and it serves as a key element in our healing process.

Mark Twain captured this phenomenon when he so succinctly stated, "The mind has a dumb sense of vast loss. That is all. It will take mind and memory months and possibly years to gather the details and know the whole extent of the loss."

On the night of Joe's death, our friends crowded into the kitchen. None of us knew what to say, so we said nothing. We simply sighed, cried and shook our heads in disbelief.

People were calling about my earlier injury and instead heard much more somber and incomprehensible news. Everyone was shocked, confused, out of balance. Mike reacted with anger and denial. His mantra throughout the eulogy and funeral was, "He is not dead. This did not happen." Nick was just plain sad. He sat on the couch with his doodle pad, drawing and erasing, for hours on hours. I can still hear the sound of the erasing mechanism, slide and click, slide and click, back and forth, again and again. Maybe he found solace in his ability to do-over, to change the outcome.

The drama of shutting my hand in the van door that morning already seemed like another lifetime though the pain and discomfort remained as a subtle reminder. Unfortunately, I had now moved far beyond an injured hand. I was certain that my heart had exploded into a million pieces. I can easily recall the devastation because for the next several years I tried to retrieve each piece in an attempt to put it all back together.

Someone in the kitchen that night mentioned that we needed to call Joe's family in New Jersey. I looked up in acknowledgement but did not volunteer. I knew that I was already past talking, past reacting and struggled with remembering to breathe. I felt irretrievably lost, somewhere deep within a vortex that was a hollow, cold and lonely place. It was as if some powerful force had sucked the life straight out of my gut, leaving a vacuous space, filled only with raw pain and anguish.

Stories from New Jersey related to us later, were equally heart wrenching. My mother called John, Joe's older and only brother. Initially she started leaving a message on their answering machine, but upon hearing her voice, he sensed there was a problem and picked up the phone. His wife Lori was putting their kids to bed and heard John scream from the bottom of the stairwell. They all ran to the stairs fearing he was physically injured, but he wasn't. The pain for him was much greater than that.

Lori's family taxied over from New York City and stayed with the kids while John and Lori left to drive across town and tell Joe's mom (Mary) about his death. They reported that she answered the door, at past midnight, probably thinking they were there to tell her that her beloved sister had died. Her sister had been sick for months and they knew she would not likely recover. Clearly, Mary could not have prepared for the news they delivered. She collapsed on the floor, inconsolable.

Back at our house, the phone kept ringing, and my mom kept saying, "He's dead, Joe's dead." Since no one believed her, she kept repeating it, sometimes even yelling at the person on the other end in an attempt to penetrate his or her confusion.

I yelled at her wanting her to stop saying those words. Pain and anguish emanated from her eyes and with the phone still in her hand, she said, "What am I supposed to say?" I shrugged dejectedly and then after a few moments quietly requested that she go into another room and close the door, so the kids did not have to keep hearing this.

At some point in that endless night, the Kittitas County coroner called, and inquired about our plans for getting "the body" back home, a distance of about 100 miles. Joe was now "the body." The transition from "Joe" to "body" was both confusing and atrocious. It is nearly impossible to wrap one's mind around this significant and instantaneous transition.

> *Regrettably, when faced with sudden death, we are unable to focus on reality. We often lose our voices as well as our ability to move or respond. Even though we continue to take in information, we are incapable of processing what we are hearing. It is as if our mind has erected an impenetrable wall, blocking out all information while simultaneously holding in the pain.*

Moaning became my most common response. For many months every time reality infiltrated my mind, I involuntarily responded by moaning. This struck me as strange, though I seemed incapable of controlling the response. Much later, another widow suggested that my moaning was probably internalized crying since I often held back my tears for the sake of the boys.

In some cultures people wail when in mourning, others (like ours) attempt to suppress displays of emotion. From my experience, wailing or something closer to that response seems to both facilitate and expedite the healing process and thus is perhaps the healthier, though less popular choice.

That night after everyone left, the boys crawled into my bed and Nick said, "Mom, are you going to die now too?" Without hesitation, Mike in an attempt to console his younger brother said, "Nick, mom's not going to die-she doesn't ride snowmobiles." Their endless and often repetitive questions about their dad, about death and about Heaven began in earnest on that first night.

After they fell asleep, I got out of bed knowing that sleep for me would not occur. I went back downstairs, back to the kitchen table. Mom had stayed over and soon joined me, watching silently while I made my list. A list that included calling family, friends and our priest, having an alarm and caller ID installed, giving away the salt-water fish tank, and hiring someone for yard services. (Somehow, I had reached 42 years of age without ever mowing a lawn). Somehow, I had already mentally prepared this list sixteen hours earlier.

I can recall only snippets of events over the next several days. Joe died on a Wednesday afternoon. Our Pastor, Father Seamus arrived on Thursday morning and by the end of the day, my parents, who divorced thirty years prior, accompanied me to the funeral home and to the cemetery.

> *In short order, we selected songs, psalms, pallbearers, a casket and a space at the Mausoleum. We ordered food, wrote an obituary and started greeting out of town guests and family members. People take months or even years to plan weddings of similar size. Unfortunately, in cases of sudden death, there are only days to make the necessary arrangements. This process is further complicated by everyone's level of shock and grief.*

The funeral home experience is challenging for families under most circumstances. However, following an unexpected death, it is also surreal because of the insufficient time to prepare, to consider options, to wrap your mind around the death and to reconcile what happened. Since we are often in a state of shock and unaccustomed to the practices and procedures of the funeral industry, having a compassionate person at the funeral home, someone who listens carefully, understands grief, and makes pertinent suggestions can better facilitate this painful process.

In retrospect, I have regretted many of the choices I made that day. There were so many details and I was not able to focus or grasp much of the incoming information. I struggle with deciphering details in optimal situations and clearly, this was a long ways from optimal.

As it was, I stumbled over decisions regarding the clothing in which to bury Joe, how to write the obituary and what type of services we should hold. At one point in our meeting, the funeral director escorted us into the casket room leaving us alone to choose. The names and prices of the caskets were on polished plaques and the piped in music played soft and low. It resembled an indoor custom car display. It felt like hell.

We held a vigil at the funeral home on Friday and the funeral followed the next morning at the church, less than 72 hours from the time of death. Joe's 82-year-old mother, his brother, sister-in-law, cousins and life-long friends arrived from the East Coast. His mother was clearly devastated and I could offer her nothing. I channeled all of my energy towards Mike and Nick, getting us through this day and with any luck, the next day as well. (In later years, whenever faced with something stressful, my mantra became "I buried my husband. What could be harder than that"?) Perspective is a useful tool.

Nick, at age four did not totally grasp the concept of death, although he understood much more than people presumed. We have a tendency in this country to underestimate our children's abilities to comprehend. However, Nick was old enough to know that his dad was gone and reportedly not coming back. He knew that everyone he loved was very sad and that we cried a lot. He knew that his life changed that day and he desperately wanted someone to change it back.

At the vigil, while someone was at the podium speaking, Nick pointed at the coffin and asked what it was. I told him what it was and that his dad was inside. He got out of his chair and tentatively approached the casket. Then he started knocking on the side of it, saying, "Hello, can you hear me?" and "Daddy, are you in there?" No one moved, as we held our collective breath. Eventually, looking confused and unsatisfied, he returned to his seat. I cannot remember what happened next. However, I recall that overall the vigil service provided only minimal comfort, compounding everyone's bewilderment.

St. Patrick's Church seats several hundred people. On the day of Joe's funeral, there were people seated on folding chairs and standing in the back. Even though the funeral was within a few days of his death, friends traveled across the country and returned from business trips as far away as Asia. Two of his closest friends and a colleague eulogized him in extraordinary fashion, yet it was John, his older brother, who penetrated the stunned crowd with an eloquent extemporaneous speech of family and brotherly love. At eight years older, he clearly recalled his joy on the day of Joe's birth and the horror on the day of Joe's death.

Following the service, family escorted Joe's mother from the church. Her grief was palpable. She had outlived her parents, all but one of her eight siblings, her husband, and most of her friends. Yet, the death of a child, of any age, is perhaps the most significant loss. Her grief was inconceivable. In a perfect world, no mother should outlive her children.

Later at the mausoleum, as the attendants attached the marble cover guarding the casket, both boys called out, "Goodbye dad, we love you" while waving, as if he were leaving for work. They looked so tragic.

"The best way out is always through"

Robert Frost

The Days that Followed

I requested copies of the accident and coroner's report for insurance purposes and because I needed to read them. The reports stated that Joe was traveling downhill at a high rate of speed and failed to negotiate a corner. His snowmobile hit a small embankment, propelling him at approximately 55 miles an hour face first into a tree. He died instantly. Brian and Jeff arrived within moments and found him collapsed in the tree well. They administered CPR for over an hour with no response. Other riders stopped to help. There was nothing more anyone could do except call for the coroner and wait.

The newspaper reported that alcohol might have been a factor and the coroner's report confirmed. Maybe this should not have mattered because the outcome remained the same. Unfortunately, for me it did matter, because the manner in which he died convoluted my grief and healing process for several years.

It was difficult, though I felt necessary, to read the formalized reports generated from Joe's accident. Seeing the words in black and white, facts neatly typed without emotion, removed any doubts that he had actually died. Deciding to read these reports was one of the more heart wrenching choices I made, though essential, since I had chosen not to view his body.

Exactly 28 days after Joe died we experienced a 6.8 earthquake. I was at work, forty-five miles from where the boys attended school. The radio reported the epicenter closer to them. I had no way of knowing the extent of damage or if they were okay. I drove through miles of non-functioning traffic lights, anxiety ridden and imagining the worst.

Sudden and unexpected death strikes at the center of the survivor's sense of stability. Since, I was already in a serious state of vulnerability this event pushed me over the top. If Joe had not died, I have little doubt that I would have reacted very differently to this earthquake.

In actuality my overall focus on life had completely narrowed to include only what remained of my immediate family. This is perhaps a common and necessary reaction because there is safety in the diminutiveness of the family unit. For the survivor anything larger can be too overwhelming.

Once again, I barreled through my mom's front door, crying, and there the boys were sitting on the floor playing cards with their grandmother. Unfortunately, for Mike, it was not a day when I could avoid crying in his presence. Fortunately, for me he found some comfort in my explanation that because they were happy tears it was okay for me to cry this time.

I quit my job that day. Partly because of what I did for a living but mostly because we needed healing time. I worked for an insurance company overseeing the settlement of liability claims. Among other things, my job included negotiating serious injury and wrongful death settlements. Ironically, one of the first claims to cross my desk after Joe died involved an Idaho woman seriously injured in a snowmobile accident.

In the six months before Joe's death, we talked about changing jobs and changing directions. He had thought about leaving his law firm and maybe going into practice with friends. I had considered changing careers altogether. We both recognized that we were at a crossroads and we agreed that changes were forthcoming.

After his death, there was little hesitation on my part to find a new career path. In addition to my job's commute time and travel requirements, my new perspective on the value of death claims was incongruous with that of my employers. I also knew that the kids and I needed time together, time I could not give them if I continued working long hours.

Two weeks later my mom told me that she had breast cancer and her surgeon had scheduled a mastectomy for the following week. I recall us sitting on the front porch, watching the kids play catch. I began to cry and in response to my tears she said, "Don't worry; I have friends who will help take care of me." I replied weakly, "Yeah, but who is going to take care of me?"

My sister Terri drove in from Yakima. She stayed with mom for a week after the surgery, splitting her time between our houses, seeing which of us most needed help. The day after Terri left, mom started hemorrhaging. I took her to the hospital and they told me that I could take her home at 9:00 p.m.

I left the hospital, started across the street and stopped midway, mindless of the passing cars. If I picked her up from the hospital at 9:00 p.m., who would be at my house making sure the kids got into bed at 7:30 p.m. I don't know how long I stood in the street. However, after several panicked phone calls to friends and family, Karen (a friend and neighbor) agreed to take Mike and Nick for me. I knew then that this was just the beginning of a very long and arduous journey, a journey I now had to make alone.

Within the next three months, my dad began radiation for prostrate cancer; my aunt underwent surgery for brain cancer and Joe's favorite aunt died. Nine months in to 2001, Mike, Nick and I sat in the living room and in horror watched the twin towers collapse. We had visited the towers several times on our New York trips and the boys thought of New York as their dad's home. I felt that the assault on our sense of safety, both inside and outside of our home, continued.

"Everyone knows they're going to die, but nobody believes it.

If we did, we would do things differently"

Morrie Schwartz

An Anticipated Death

An anticipated death first occurs when you are informed by a doctor that you have a potentially life ending disease for which there is no cure. Customarily, until that single defining moment when we learn of this disease we have not spent much time planning for or in anticipation of our own death. Our level of anxiety can vary depending on what the doctor tells us about the disease and possible treatments as well as our ability to assimilate this information.

I have spoken with people shortly after first learning of their potential life ending diagnosis, and their physical and emotional reactions sound similar to the response when learning of a sudden death, suggesting that shock is a dominant component in both situations. The reactions described included the over-reactive heartbeat pounding in their ears so loudly that it drowns out all other sounds, coupled with an inability to focus or respond and followed by panic, doubt and disbelief.

> *Yet, it is at this time when we must make crucial decisions pertaining to medical interventions while firmly embedded in a state of shock. We have questions without answers, fears without reprieve, and are recipients of an unrelenting avalanche of medical jargon. A spouse who had encountered this experience accurately reflected that it was much like trying to take a drink of water from a fire hose.*

The many medical specialists encountered, frequently offer new and at times, conflicting information. At this profoundly difficult time, we face a myriad of choices including surgery, chemotherapy, radiation, medical trials and a slew of medications. Throughout this chaos, we depend on our doctors for an accurate prediction of remission versus reoccurrence, quality versus quantity, and life versus death.

Couples relate stories of arriving home, holding each other, crying, staring vacantly at nothing in particular and asking, why them and why now. They know that they have to call family and friends and let everyone know about the diagnosis. They often know in advance how some will react.

If judgments are forthcoming, they often materialize at that time. Friends and family members remind lung cancer patients that they should not have smoked and they remind liver failure patients that they should not have consumed alcohol or drugs. This information is not particularly germane or helpful. Yet, that does not prevent these recriminating statements and stating them seems to be inherent for some people.

The helpers, while not judgmental, comprise yet another category of respondents. They immediately engage their computers in search of information on the disease and the prognosis, searching for common as well as uncommon avenues of treatment, all the while hoping and/or praying for a positive outcome. They seek out other people with similar diagnosis to ascertain which treatments worked and ultimately, how they survived. Their intentions are good though at times appear intrusive. They too are experiencing some modicum of fear, confusion, and a sense of futility.

For the patient and the family bad news often arrives in stages, each setback further weakening everyone's resolve. The surgeons operate with the expectation of full recovery. Regimens of chemotherapy or radiation commence and for a while, there is a focal point of hope for a cure or at least for more time. In our confusion, we often think that treatable means curable. Regrettably, new or different symptoms appear or the doctor finds evidence of the tumor's reoccurrence.

The fear and diminished morale resurface, each time eroding hope, until that day when all options are exhausted. Now only one choice remains– all involved must begin the process of digesting and accepting the finality of the prognosis.

On those occasions when the progression or the nature of the disease preclude any treatment options at all, the doctors can only say they are sorry, and send the patients home to get their affairs in order, and perhaps call hospice.

Eventually most people in anticipation of their death arrive at this place of reckoning, whether it takes weeks, months or years. The length of intervening time between diagnosis and death often dictates the speed and symmetry of each person's customized roller coaster ride, whether slow and purposeful or fast and furious, sometimes within our control and other times not. Regrettably, there are occasions when all we have time to do is close our eyes, hold on tight, and hope for the best.

Men and women often accept a terminal diagnosis differently. One reason is that women possess an innate sense of care giving and conversely are generally not reluctant to allow others to care for them. In contrast, men are generally not predisposed as either caregivers or recipients of care giving. Unfortunately, for many the act of dying demands that we relinquish much of our independence as well as our social identity.

The spectrum of the losses we incur can include forced retirement, the inability to drive and decreased physical stamina affecting both recreational pursuits and household chores. We have insufficient energy to attend social/community events and we experience the loss of capacity for self-care such as bathing, shaving and eating. Occasionally these profound losses occur over an extended period, however, depending on the disease process, some of us are required to abandon all of these activities on incredibly short notice. The accompanying shock and sense of loss when this occurs is profoundly overwhelming.

We should not be surprised when people who are dying, especially those who were physically active before their illness, become agitated, angry and depressed. Is it also not surprising when people in careers that require control and command such as airline pilots, engineers, judges, teachers and ministers, to name a few, struggle more because of their inability to control their disease process.

It is important to remember that while we are saying goodbye to our companion and foreseeing the end of that relationship, they are saying goodbye to us and to everyone and everything they have known in this life. Our loss is individual and their loss is all-encompassing. We cannot know what this experience is like for them.

Even though our companions have already incurred many physical losses throughout the course of their illness, their emotions remain intact and often in a state of chaos. It therefore becomes our task to acknowledge these emotions. We can do this best through an inordinate amount of patience and by staying focused on what each of us is experiencing.

"Grief is a crisis not only of overwhelming emotion but of daily interaction and identity."

Author Unknown

Anticipatory Grief

Whether you are the patient or the spouse, anticipatory grief is something akin to grieving in expectation of the actual death. It is when you begin to realize that because of this newly discovered disease, your lifestyle, your relationships and possibly your belief systems are in the process of a radical and permanent change. Unfortunately, there is no road map and much of the anxiety stems from not knowing what is going to happen.

This shift in focus takes time to occur and to digest. Therefore, if the disease progression is rapid you may not have the opportunity to experience much anticipatory grief, because you can't get past the shock. Conversely, if you have time to adjust, you start seeing how this loss will affect you while simultaneously grieving the life you had been living, before the diagnosis. Processing this information often includes a thorough examination of your present situation and of your available options.

As the primary caregiver, you slowly begin to acquire your spouse's role within the family and his work within the household, making it look temporary for everyone's benefit, yet on some level you know differently. During this time, you reside in alternate realities. In one, you continue your spousal relationship while offering comfort, hope and companionship. In the other, you continue to look toward the months ahead speculating about the forthcoming changes in your life.

Thus, while exerting enormous amounts of physical and emotional energy, your thoughts remain focused on what your life is going to look like next week or next year. Some of you wonder how you will afford to pay the bills once his income stops. You may consider selling the house, taking in a tenant or contemplate new employment opportunities.

There are multiple considerations, which vary significantly depending on your relationship, age, financial status, employment and many more factors. You may opt not to discuss any of this with your dying partner because you do not want to cause any added grief or concern and because even thinking about it might feel disloyal.

However, maintaining these opposing dialogues, the one in your mind, unstated, and those you feel free to discuss with your spouse can increase your level of anxiety and exhaustion. Simultaneously, your spouse probably also maintains dual dialogues. He likely struggles with accepting the inevitable and at the same time hesitates to share his fears and concerns with you.

Acceptance and awareness span the spectrum and for most people it becomes a moving target. Some people when dying maintain denial throughout the entire process and some people accept death as a natural progression of life, at times asking only for spiritual or emotional support and stamina. For many people the levels of acceptance and understanding fall somewhere between these two points and change frequently.

In addition, your emotions as well as their intensity vary from day to day. When your spouse is dying you both experience variations of shock, denial, anger, depression and acceptance. Some people move from one emotion to the other and back again and some people remain frozen in place. This manner of processing is normal and necessary. There is no set pattern or schedule to grief. Each of us is unique and we respond to loss in our own way.

For those who are able to transcend the shock, even temporarily, anticipatory grief allows you to glean a modicum of acceptance, understanding and closure. In this acknowledgment, there exists opportunities for resolving conflicts, for making amends and for saying goodbyes.[1]

Most significantly, there exists the opportunity for your spouse to share his fears, concerns and love, for your family to share memories and create new ones. Through open communication, the dying individual has the chance to teach others about courage and grace, which ultimately gives him and everyone around him a measure of peace. These are the gifts made possible by an anticipated death.

However, not everyone reaches this level of awareness, especially if because of circumstances or beliefs, they did not fully understand that death was inevitable. There is no right or wrong, good or bad, only what happens and why, and understanding how or why something happens makes adjusting and ultimately accepting the outcome easier for everyone involved.

In a 1959 play by Samuel Beckett, Jean Anouilh stated, "Until the day of his death, no man can be sure of his courage." Fighting to live until the moment of death takes much courage. This is especially evident when considering the harshness of the disease fighting treatments - surgeries, radiation, chemotherapy and other pungent medications.

Accepting and acknowledging death also requires courage. Hospital and hospice workers witness courageous acts of the dying and their family members every day, regardless of their resolve. In truth many of us have not yet considered, or at least remain unsure, how we will approach our own deaths. This, I believe, is human nature.

Some people die in the midst of treatment or on their way back to the hospital or the doctor's office. If neither of you acknowledged that your spouse was dying, it is possible that no one activated or identified by name, the act of care giving. Simply stated, care giving is taking care of a sick or dying individual, though there is nothing simple about the act itself.

Anticipatory grief is much the same, because even if neither of you believed that death was imminent, the diagnosis alone resulted in a shift in how you previously viewed your world and lived your life. The diagnosis itself unlocked the doors of anticipatory grief, regardless of your understanding, acknowledgement or preparation for what was happening.

Since most often, neither you nor your spouse had prior experience with the dying process or the accompanying emotional upheaval, one of your greatest challenges was maintaining any semblance of normalcy. It is not easy to maintain normalcy in chaos. As your spouse is dying, your world is collapsing around you, the house is a mess and no one has the energy or time to cook dinner. Even when someone delivers food, no one is particularly interested in eating. It is at this point that grief and loss become more familiar, while the normal events of your daily lives become less so.

*"Only a life lived for others
is a life worthwhile"*

Albert Einstein

Caring for your Dying Spouse

Taking care of your dying spouse does not feel like a normal experience and is probably not something you envisioned on your wedding day, even though you may have vowed, "until death do us part." However, since dying together is not customary, one of you is destined to acquire the role of caregiver. In your experience as a care-giving spouse, you learn that death is the great equalizer, immune to race, gender, age, wealth, status, education or the depth of your love.

Your encounter with spousal care giving depends on a multitude of factors, including your relationship, family dynamics, family and community support, communication and the disease process itself. If your spouse was in ill health for an extended period, you may have suffered from caregiver burn out even before this final prognosis. Regardless of your stamina or desire to help, everyone has a limit.

There often exists a sense of immortality with a long-standing terminal prognosis. There may have been multiple times when the doctors thought and conveyed that death was near, however somehow he survived and stabilized and at some point, everyone stopped believing in that prognosis, and reverted to that irrational belief in immortality. As a result, when death actually occured no one was prepared.

Often as the spouse and primary caregiver, you feel guilty for not believing or for not seeing the signs of an approaching death. However, if your spouse fails to speak up or take note, how could you have, and if you had noticed, would anything be different now? Try not to punish yourself for being human. Instead, remember that you walked beside your spouse providing loving and caring support at the most challenging point of your relationship and probably the most difficult time of your lives. In essence, you both did your best under the circumstances.

The existence of family and community support greatly influences your ability to provide care for your dying spouse. It is nearly impossible, though unfortunately common, for one person to provide all of the care giving. It is much better for all concerned if there are two or more full time caregivers, because as you now know, living with someone who is dying is physically, emotionally and spiritually exhausting. You frequently skip meals, fluid intake, and sleep. One caregiver responded that she was too tired to sleep, an observation, which undoubtedly resonates with many of you.

Invariably, before one's spouse dies, almost all solo caregivers reach a point where they believe that they cannot continue. If you feel that you dissolved prematurely and were unable to provide the level of care you felt was necessary, it is vital at this time to forgive yourself for both real and perceived lapses in care giving. Everyone has limits and those limits vary from one person to another, regardless of your intent.

At the onset, most caregivers cannot know how difficult taking care of their dying companion is going to be, which means there is usually a component of panic. Everyone has different coping mechanisms, which are at times further eroded by family dynamics and by the illness itself. I would roughly estimate that 10% of all caregivers experience a great deal of chaos and crisis, 10% experience a rather peaceful event, and 80% fall somewhere in between.

The decline of your spouse's health likely occurred over a period of many weeks or months while the world outside kept going on seemingly unaffected. This normalcy of the outer world is difficult to digest because your spouse's illness turns your lives upside down and inside out. Your focus is on keeping him emotionally and physically comfortable, a feat that is nearly impossible considering the disease process and the chemicals used to treat them. The disease and the treatment have the potential to alter his personality, your interaction and ultimately the nature of your relationship. An important caregiver mantra is, "This is the disease talking, not my spouse."

The truth is that, until you live with someone who is dying, you cannot possibly know what is involved or the extent of difficulties you may incur. I hope that if you had assistance in place, it proved sufficient to ease your spouse's symptoms and the care giving burdens for you. One older caregiver said that he thought taking care of his dying wife was going to be like a ride on a Ferris wheel, doing the same thing day after day, in slow motion, with a nearly imperceptible decline. Unfortunately to his surprise, taking care of her ended up being more like a ride on a roller coaster, with rapid changes and unpredicted trepidation.

Hospice workers often talk about the invariable similarities between coming in to this world and leaving it. Not knowing when or how the birth or death will occur, exemplifies the lack of control humans have over nature. The intensity of care required for ill and healthy newborns rivals the intensity of care for the dying. Often neither the newborn nor the dying individual is capable of expressing their needs, their pains or their thoughts. As a new parent and as a caregiver you often guess, stress, laugh and cry and in the end, you did the best that you could.

Obviously, the difference between being born and dying is that the former event represents a joyous occasion, a new life and a new relationship while the latter event signifies an unhappy occasion, the ending of a life and a significantly altered relationship.

When a death is prolonged requiring intensive care giving, you may feel a sense of relief at the time of death and as a result, your psychological health improves.[2] However, (important note here) this does not preclude you from missing your spouse after he dies. Nor does it prevent you from grieving the end of your dreams and plans, including among other things, spending many more years together.

Frequently, spouses surviving an anticipated death report that their level of grief surprises them because they feel that they were adequately prepared by the time the death occurred, thus decreasing the severity and duration of grief. However, accepting the death and adjusting to the end of your relationship, as you knew it, are two different things and the former does not always influence the latter. Your spouse's death is manifested by his physical absence from your every day life. You may have just lost your best friend or your only friend, and adjusting to that is not easy.

For people experiencing a lingering death, their dying journey is often distressing and lonely. In America, the number of aged has rapidly increased. We also live in a period where society is exceedingly mobile, resulting in separation and/or alienation from primary family members. As a result, many older spouses face caring for their loved one alone or the dying face the choice of relocating to a nursing home, if economically feasible, because their companion is not physically able to care for them.

As you may now know, people no longer stay in hospitals to die. Once your spouse's symptoms stabilized, the hospital discharged him home. This may have been quite a shock since you envisioned dying quite differently. This is where the assistance of multiple family members or caring friends becomes crucial or conversely where you realize how alone you really are. People often express shock at this time at the cost of hired care giving or nursing homes. The cost is too much for most of us and thus we end up trying to provide sufficient care at home and at times, alone.

Occasionally dying individuals summon former spouses to provide end-of-life care giving. Usually this occurs when a modicum of friendship survived the divorce and no other family members are available to help. In addition, many companions must take on all of the care giving responsibilities because they have limited community and family resources or they are isolated within their relationship.

In situations where the caregiver spouse still works, there is often no one available to care for the ill spouse, especially if continued employment is paramount for maintaining medical insurance or if not working equates to no income. This factor adds stress to an already challenging situation when considering the complexities in adequately caring for a dying spouse, absorbing the onslaught of emotions, fulfilling your employment obligations, taking care of the household and managing self-care.

Though there have been reports of enhanced awareness, we still have much work ahead of us in educating employers and government agencies about the stressors associated with caring for a dying companion, in today's society.

If you have time to assimilate, what is actually hap-pening, your transformation from denial to acceptance is evident. Often by the time death occurs, everyone is ready to let go. Whether letting go of life or the relationship, con-trol or resistance, many of us reach a level of acceptance in recognizing death as the only possible outcome, the only resolution for ending the suffering.

In caring for your spouse during his dying journey, you may have had many opportunities to communicate your feelings through talk and touch. Even though you did not envision this ending on your wedding day or throughout your relationship, caring for your dying spouse pro-vided opportunity for meaningful interaction and the ultimate bonding experience.

"The question is not whether we will die, but how we will live."

Joan Borysenko

Chuck's Story

In hospice work, we encounter a wide-ranging cross section of people. Many of them have led remarkable lives and approach death in a similar fashion. One experience stands out, going beyond the ordinary, both because of the length of time we were associated and because of the depth of our newly formed friendship. Within moments of meeting Chuck, I knew that he would die as he lived, in memorable fashion.

Chuck was small in stature yet large in spirit. He was incredibly honest, faith - filled and family oriented. He was a significant member of his community and thus struggled with the fact that I lived outside of that community. In our first meeting, he repeatedly brought up this fact, and questioned whether he could convince me to move.

His initial diagnosis of cancer came in 1993. While playing tennis Chuck felt three lumps on the right side of his neck. After a quick consult, his doctor sent him to Virginia Mason in Seattle. Initial rounds of radiation and chemotherapy were effective. However, three years later the doctors diagnosed a new cancer and he again treated with radiation.

Although, initially successful, six years later his disease process required that he undergo a tracheotomy. At this point, because the doctors believed that he had less than six months to live, they suggested hospice. However, Chuck's condition stabilized for three more years until September of 2005 when for a second and final time they told him that it was time to go home, get his affairs in order and call hospice.

According to his wife, Tina, after that first diagnosis, Chuck felt like his life did not belong to him any longer. There was him and there was the cancer, and he never knew which of them were in control. Even though he was strong in his faith, sometimes that was not enough. He set short-term goals because the future was tenuous. However, in the thirteen years from his initial diagnosis to his death, he managed to accomplish many of these goals.

Because of his tracheotomy, his speech was at times difficult to understand. This made our visits even more intriguing when combined with the emotional energy expended when talking candidly with someone who is dying. Tina would come home from work to assist in the communication process. She did this because it was important for her to participate in every aspect of Chuck's dying journey.

Chuck and Tina had enjoyed a thirty-nine year marriage, complete with children, family gatherings, an always-open door, many friends and of course, tennis. Tennis was one of Chuck's four greatest passions in life, intermingled with family, faith and his community. Early on, he told people that he was prepared to die because he had already scheduled a tennis match in heaven with Arthur Ashe.

His primary concern during our first meeting was that he would not die before Thanksgiving. He felt this would result in his family having to cancel their family reunion in Texas. What soon became clear in our conversations was that Chuck had a plan, and since he had worked as an architectural engineer, plans were important to him.

Thankfully, Chuck's cancer reached a plateau by Thanksgiving so the entire family boarded a plane and flew south. They looked forward to visiting the towns where they had lived, other family members and old friends. On return, he mentioned that it would be especially nice if he could live long enough to see the Rose Bowl since the University of Texas was playing. Translated, this meant that Chuck was feeling better and as a result, he had revised his plan.

Chuck never asked anyone to pray for his recovery. However, he asked that everyone pray for his psychological and spiritual strength at that moment and as his disease progressed. He was more at peace with his dying process than most people, which in turn made everyone around him more comfortable. His spiritual strength was unyielding and contagious.

Anyone who spent time with Chuck grew more attached, more entwined in his family. Often his sisters would visit and they would hold family conferences around a food-filled table. Perhaps this was bittersweet for Chuck since he could no longer eat.

On one occasion, his daughter asked him to write her a letter about their relationship, about his disease, his life and his impending death. Instead, Chuck wrote her a letter about how much he enjoyed his hospice team. This was his way of teasing her, and it worked. Although with minimal delay, he wrote her the letters she had wanted.

On one particularly cold and wet day in mid December, Chuck called in apparent distress. I struggled with comprehending what he was saying, since I was unable to watch his lips and in his panic, he was more difficult to understand. Tina entered the conversation and confirmed, sadly, that their son-in-law had died, the victim of a homicide. Chuck asked us to meet him at his daughter's house, hoping that we could help him help her.

This tragic experience interfered with Chuck's plan. Dying now was more complicated because his daughter needed him alive and because no one in his family needed another death. Now there was a new and significant twist to both his grieving process and his preparedness to die.

For a while, Chuck quit talking about dying. Instead, he created a massive "to do" list. This list encompassed decades of disregarded household repairs and improvements. He had good reason for not having completed these chores: he was busy playing tennis. According to his wife, Chuck played tennis every free moment, and since family was important, they played tennis with him. It was on the tennis court where he first discovered the lumps in his neck, and it was subsequently on the tennis court where we eulogized him.

One day, his hospice nurse, Helen called to report that Chuck had decided to remove a kitchen wall. Helen looked at the kitchen, minus all of the appliances and counters, and said something like, "Wow, you and Tina really took on a project here," to which he replied, "Tina doesn't know about it yet, but I think she'll like it." Helen was still laughing when she reported the conversation much later in the day.

Chuck's family continued their healing process and Chuck's disease process remained unchanged, as he meticulously worked his list, item by item. Appearing at his house proved interesting if you did not have time to help because there was always something to move, lift, shift, paint or nail down. His son finally threw up his hands, stating he could not stay there all day, every day. He had his house, his job and his own family to consider. Chuck was obviously obsessed with his list, leaving everyone to wonder what he would do once his list was completed.

In "*A Story of Heroes, Healing and Hope*" published by the Virginia Mason Cancer Center in 1998, Chuck relayed that having cancer was the best thing that ever happened to him. He was quoted as saying, "For 35 years I ignored God, but when I got cancer, I found a new source of spirituality, and developed a faith that carried me through. And I learned that I had to accept dying before I could really live." Chuck was one of those rare people who not only spoke his faith but also lived his faith.

Nine months after initiating hospice care, Chuck began his slow and purposeful decline. He began questioning in earnest how much longer he had to live and why he was still alive in the first place. Of course, no one had the answer, only calculated guesses. This of course was inadequate data for an architect who required detailed plans. Maybe his final lesson in life was to learn that dying was the one event he could not plan or maybe his family needed more time to prepare for his death. We could only speculate.

As he approached death, Tina wrote the following journal entry, which I believe captures an accurate slice of what was happening. She was exhausted, having not slept much for days and she wrote quickly in hopes of capturing it all. It read:

> "*Since early morning 4:30 ish, Chuck's motor skills appear different. I kept thinking he wanted the notebook and pen to write. It was that kind of motion. His lips moving, eyes staring at the ceiling, several times as if he was talking.*
>
> *During the evening, he'd look to my side as if someone was there. I'd say no one was there, but he'd reach out as to touch the invisible person or shadow. I'd tell him everyone was gone. Then he'd wave like okay.*
>
> *It's 6:00 now and his eyes continued staring at the ceiling with pleasant, clear eyes and intensity. He played with his finger as if he has something, his lips occasionally moving. I truly feel like I shouldn't be in this room. Very*

*strange after spending almost 31 years in here, in this bed-
room, a "private thing" is happening.*

*I remembered the "Journey's End" booklet about how
sometimes a person dies when you just went out of the
room for a while. Well, I felt it was time to give him privacy. Very strange. Almost like the "changing of the guard."*

*With the candle flickering at my table and a cup of
coffee, I wait.*

*There is a calmness to me but with sadness that Chuck
is leaving soon, and I want to go with him, but it's not my
turn. That's how I'm developing my patience, "It's not my
turn," and waiting makes some people stronger and others
angry. I'm not sure where I'm at now, but I know I must
wait.*

*I want to go back into the room, open the door, but
I'm scared to interrupt a passage of time.*

*I waited 34 minutes before returning to the room. He
had scooted to the end of the bed. When he saw me he was
happy, but instantly his eyes roamed to the right, then to
the left. His stare became transitional as if he was passing
through, astonishing, curious, very observant…hard to explain. When I had left the room, he was/his body was very
cold. When I returned his body was warm to the touch. He
appeared to want to write so I passed him the notebook but
that's not what he wanted.*

*I swear he was writing to GOD or a very significant
being. His hands and fingers were in writing position w/
the index finger and thumb holding an imaginary pen."*

Chuck died the next morning. Many observed some of the activities
Tina wrote about while sitting with him in his final days and hours.
To all, it was clear that he was communicating with someone, or some-
thing, that only he could see.

Chuck was truly a great man, and I am confident that all who knew
him considered themselves fortunate to have spent time in his presence.
We talked about the Hindi word "Namaste" which to my understanding means, "The spirit in me honors the spirit in you." Chuck's spirit

touched and recognized everyone who spent quality time with him. Even though Tina knew he was dying and even though all of his family was ready to let him die, his physical absence from their lives fast became paramount. Approximately three months following Chuck's death, Tina wrote:

> *"There are so many things I want to talk about but only to Chuck. I am not asking for answers or explanations. I just need to tell Chuck things…He is the one I trusted with all my heart."*

And, she later shared this reflective poem:

Dancing cheek to cheek is what I wish for us tonight
Dancing 'till the music stops
The smell of the Tropicana roses is what I wish to smell tonight
The roses you so loved
I miss your smell, so I cling to one shirt
To feel you here tonight
But the music has stopped
Dancing cheek to cheek is only an illusion
The roses have died
And your smell has faded
And taken us our separate ways."

*"All men think all men
mortal but themselves"*

Edward Young

Accepting Mortality

Many widows in retrospect relate feelings of confusion, frustration and guilt about some of the decisions they made regarding treatment options. They question the correctness of these choices, concerned that these choices may have negatively influenced the quality or the quantity of their spouse's remaining days. It is therefore necessary to discuss the possible motivation behind the choices made, choices that can later become the foundation for resultant misgivings.

> *In America we are poorly informed and often in denial about matters surrounding death and dying. In part, this stems from the simple fact that none of us long for or look forward to this final stage of life. Even if our lives have been less than rewarding, we have grown comfortable with our laws of nature and with our existential existence. Death, for many represents the unknown or at least a significant transformation, both requiring certain bravado.*

For others, actual death instills no fear, yet the dying process itself causes many of us much angst. Thus, because death and dying evoke these and other negative emotions, our natural response becomes one of denial or at least avoidance. We try to out run or out fox the disease process, hoping in vain to alter or at least delay the inevitable.

Until perhaps the 1940's, death was a common household occurrence in America. There were no antibiotics, there were few cures and the average life span was much shorter. Family members fully experienced, in their homes, the deaths of babies and grandparents, brothers and sisters, moms and dads.

Rituals and customs such as draping the front door in black signaled neighbors and even strangers walking by that a family member had died. At these times, it was appropriate for members of the community to enter the home and pay their final respects to the deceased. The families prepared their loved one's bodies, which remained in the home until burial.

Then antibiotics and other medical advances emerged and death shifted from the home to the hospital, nursing home or funeral parlor. We no longer witnessed the dying process. Instead, the hospital staff assured total isolation and separation from disease and death by limiting visiting hours. Television and movies promoted death as being clean, quick and easy. Americans began the process of forgetting that death was in fact a natural progression of life.

Because of this shift, there currently exists a lack of awareness in this country and insufficient education around the dying process coupled with an overall avoidance of mortality. This enigma manifests itself as nothing less than a disengagement from the reality that all living things must die. Part of the problem rests with human nature, since focusing on death and dying would be counterproductive to enjoying and living life. However, we continue to devote unlimited resources toward extending life while simultaneously avoiding discussions around death and dying.

Unfortunately, we have now created a cocoon wherein the human capacity for self-deception regarding death is almost infinite.[3]   "The definition of science and technology has led us to believe that inevitably they could overcome all problems, negativity, suffering, and inconvenience in human life; that finally, medical science might even find a cure for death."[4] Many Americans have either never comprehended or have since forgotten that death is unavoidable.

Regrettably, since the process of death and dying is an event we only do once, we often struggle with our choices and frequently delay making necessary decisions until we reach a crisis state.

Ultimately, the crises multiply and crash over each other, leaving patients and their families without an adequate knowledge base or sufficient opportunity to resolve them. "Studies suggested that medical care for patients with serious and advanced illnesses illustrated the under-treatment of symptoms, conflicts about who should make decisions about the patient's care, impairments in caregivers' physical and psychological health, and depletion of family resources."[5] Americans, who are dying, as well as their families, lack an understanding about both medical and care-giving options. Each of us would benefit from education on end-of-life care, including learning about withdrawal of life support and life sustaining measures.

As a culture, we need to shed the taboo surrounding the subject of death instead of erecting impenetrable walls of denial. The crucial message conveyed in the tragedy of the publicized deaths of Nancy Cruzan and Terri Schiavo was that even in our twenties and thirties we need to give consideration and voice to our desires and concerns around death and dying. These decisions will most likely change as we age, making it imperative that we continue these introspections and discussions and revise our plans when necessary.

Upon learning of a life ending diagnosis, researchers recommended emphasizing advance care planning rather than promoting advanced directives or living wills.[6] Advance care planning includes issues such as identifying caregivers, selecting guardians for minor children and making decisions around life support. In essence, advance care planning includes issues involving life support versus comfort measures and making choices between staying home versus relocating to a hospice house or a nursing home. Planning gives us the opportunity to determine now how we would like to live at the end of our lives and in doing so how we are ultimately going to experience death.

A recent study concluded that thirty-three percent of married couples would not choose their spouse as their medical proxy– to make decisions on their behalf should they become incapacitated. The explanation given was that either they wanted to avoid burdening their spouse with having to make these decisions or they felt their spouse would not honor their wishes.[7] This study corroborated the significance of spouses engaging in candid conversation regarding preferences for treatment at the end of life.

Ernest Morgan stated, "Confronting death has the paradoxical effect of enriching life." Unfortunately couples often avoid talking about their concerns and fears in a futile attempt to spare each other's feelings, though I have never heard anyone express regret for having had this conversation. Most people prefer that their dying spouse make their own end of life decisions because it is extremely difficult and painful when we must make these decisions on their behalf.

Hospital workers will tell you that it is common for the family to gather in the hallways, in full understanding of what is happening to their loved one, while he struggles alone in his room, worried about his family.

When the two come back together, they often deny the truth, as well as their feelings. Instead, they talk only of remittance and cures, all in an attempt to spare each other's feelings. "Family communication patterns may change during terminal illness. Families may communicate less in order to protect each other from the reality of death."[8] True grace occurs when someone or something brings the family members together in acknowledgment and acceptance of what is actually happening, which allows everyone the opportunity to grieve together and to say goodbye.

A doctor's candor regarding treatment options and probable outcomes is essential if we wish to establish a plan. If the physicians are not completely candid then we create and initiate plans around events that are not going to occur and this generates frustration and intensifies anxiety. "Everyone must die. If that is the given and inescapable end of all human life, no matter what doctors do, then maybe we would be healthier as a society if we would embrace the inevitable rather than pushing against it."[9] In my opinion, the healthiest reaction calls for us to embrace dying once it becomes inevitable. Stated more succinctly, once there is nothing left to fight against or fight with; it is perhaps time to stop fighting.

"There is a dignity in dying that doctors should not dare to deny"

Author Unknown

The Medical Maze

Doctors trained and educated in the western-medical model have focused the majority, if not all, of their skills on managing symptoms and on delaying death. For obvious reasons they struggle with having to look their patients in the eye and tell them they have a life-ending disease for which there is no cure. Doctors must continually balance treatment options and probable outcomes with the personal cost to the patient and their family members. The patient's natural inclination to seek treatment in hopes of delaying their death can further complicate this balancing act.

When the topic of conversation is a life ending diagnosis, it is vital that we receive legitimate information on our prognosis and treatment options. Including, how these options will affect our prognosis and ultimately our quality of life. Additionally, we deserve compassionate treatment, coupled with a definitive acceptance of this prognosis by our doctors.

Thus, in order to transform how Americans behave toward death and dying, further education of the medical community is paramount. Viewing death as failure is especially true among members of the medical profession.[10] A doctor who instructs other doctors on delivering death messages in emergency rooms starts his presentation by telling the physicians in his audience that they and everyone they know are going to die.[11] What is both startling and revealing about this information is that it requires conveyance in the first place, implying that doctors do not consciously acknowledge mortality.

Hospice administrators expend a great amount of energy educating medical professionals because of the bias of physicians toward curative treatment measures even when a cure is not likely. "Death, once viewed as a natural and expected milestone of human existence, has been transformed into an unwanted outcome of disease."[12] What must occur is a transformation of the way physicians view death by understanding and ultimately accepting that death is the natural progression of life.

"There are many reasons why patients who have advanced illnesses receive inadequate care, but most of those reasons are rooted in a medical philosophy that remains focused almost exclusively on curing illness and prolonging life, rather than on improving the quality of life and relieving suffering."[13]

> *Ideally, doctors, hospitals, insurers and hospice agencies would best serve people who are dying by finding a balance between the doctors' need to provide curative measures with the patients' right to receive comfort measures.*

This is especially true when talking about younger people. For obvious reasons, an early death is more difficult for everyone to understand and accept. As such, neither doctors nor patients want anyone to think that they gave up prematurely. Unfortunately, this line of thinking often results in unnecessary treatment and late or no referrals for comfort measures for younger patients and their families. Granted there are multiple variables and frequently doctors have no way of knowing in which direction or at what speed the disease is progressing.

"Far too many patients die who were never referred for hospice care. This is often the result of an unawareness of hospice and palliative care programs by patients and their families. This lack of knowledge or awareness of compassionate end-of-life care can lead to tragic and unnecessary pain and suffering— physical, emotional and spiritual— for the patient and their families."[14]

Elderly patients also die while in the process of receiving invasive treatment that is not likely to enhance their quality or quantity of life. This trend exemplifies the broader scoped problem— our society's denial that death is the natural outcome of life. Resolution of this issue will occur only with candid discussion and increased awareness on everyone's part - a discussion that needs to acknowledge cultural, religious, ethical and moral issues.

Physicians' inability to predict the time of death (prognosticate) accurately also contributes to unnecessary treatment and delayed hospice or palliative care referrals. "Prognostication at the end of life is difficult for physicians because there is currently a dearth of evidence-based research to guide them in this effort."[15]

In other words, the process of determining when a person may die is further complicated by an explosion of newly developed medications and medical procedures, which have not existed long enough to have an established record of accomplishment in extending or improving life. Additionally, many new and rare diseases are emerging– diseases that do not have a known trajectory.

Reports from the hearing before the Special Committee on Aging in the United States Senate on September 18, 2000 reflected that the physician's prognosis regarding the amount of time the patient would live were accurate only 20% of time, and in fact, they overestimated by more than a factor of five.[16] An illustration of this finding would be a doctor telling a patient that she had five months to live, dying one month later. We can assume that some of this over-estimating is a direct result of hope, as well as an overwhelming desire to help, to fix, and ultimately to save.

Unfortunately, these aspirations often interfere with reality. "Despite broad agreement that home-based, symptom-guided care is the preferred form of medical care at the end of life, approximately half of all Medicare beneficiaries die in acute care hospitals rather than at home."[17] Death in the emergency room or acute care centers often occurs because patients have been not been told or do not believe that they are actually dying. As a result, they spend their final days traveling by ambulance between their home and the hospital.

It is the ultimate responsibility of the physician to recognize and acknowledge that a person's life is ending and that no viable treatment options remain that will postpone death, while simultaneously providing the patient with a tolerable quality of life. In the business world, they might call this the point of diminishing returns. "When patients are dying, doctors need to bring their expertise to the table

> *and help families to choose treatment options— especially when the choice of NO treatment is the best option."* [18]

In essence, there exists no universally accepted definition for the term 'end-of-life' as it pertains to a specific amount of time, versus an exact time of death. However, several components comprise that time of life when end-of-life care begins, including the presence of an incurable disease. "In clinical medicine, the 'end-of-life' can be thought of as the time period preceding an individual's natural death from a process that is unlikely to be arrested by medical care."[19] Since prognosis varies by disease and by individual, the amount of time spent dying also varies.[20]

> *Therefore, it is not practical, nor necessary, to determine a specific period when end-of-life begins. What is practical and necessary is for us to plan for our ultimate demise in the same manner as we plan for other major life events, such as marriage, bearing children, college and retirement. In preparation for dying, this includes wills, advanced planning, life insurance, and designating guardians for your minor children.*

A recently released study conducted by Dartmouth Medical School revealed that, "There is growing concern about the way chronic illness is managed in the United States, and about the possibility that some chronically ill and dying Americans might be receiving too much care— more than they and their families actually want or benefit from."[21] The crucial question being: If the doctors provided patients with accurate information about their diagnosis, prognosis, and how the treatments would ultimately affect this prognosis, would the patients choose to treat up until their moment of death?

We all have the irrefutable right to choose how we are going to approach the end of our lives. However, receiving erroneous information regarding treatment options and prognosis can result in misguided decisions. "It is possible through education, open discussion, and empowerment that people can reclaim the process of dying as their own."[22] Some people want to literally die fighting and choose quantity of life over quality of life. I support their right to make this decision as long as their physicians relayed sufficient information to them regarding their options and the probable outcomes.

Data has revealed that of all Americans who died in 2002, 25% died at home, 25% died in a nursing facility, and 50% died in the hospital or in acute care.[23] We can assume that some of the 50% who died in the hospital or acute care were from injuries or sudden onset illnesses. The actual number of patients represented in this 50% figure and how they died is the unknown factor. It would be interesting to ascertain how many of the 50% had been diagnosed with a life ending disease and how many of them actually understood they were dying.

After learning of the terminal diagnosis, we make decisions based on our individual perceptions, our cultural upbringing or religious convictions and our trust in the medical community. In retrospect, no amount of second-guessing can alter the decisions made or the resulting outcomes. You simply did the best that you could with what you knew at that time.

"What we have once enjoyed,
we can never lose.
All that we love
deeply becomes a part of us."

Helen Keller

The Elements of Grief

The single most important thing you can understand about grief is that no two people experience grief in the same way. Giving yourself permission to grieve your way is the greatest gift you can give yourself. Allowing others to grieve their way is the greatest gift you can give them. There is no universally correct manner in which to express grief. In searching, and at times in desperation, you will find your own way.

The emotions of grief can include anger, fear, disbelief, anxiety, guilt, sorrow loneliness, shock and numbness among others. You may experience behavioral changes including a significant change in appetite, recurrent crying, an inability to perform simple tasks, restlessness, disruption of thought patterns, indifference to the world around you, social withdrawal, disrupted sleep and disturbing dreams.

Physical pain is an element of grief that many find surprising. Often the pain centers in the stomach. Other times people feel as though their hearts have literally broken - they ache and feel constricted in some fashion. Many widows find themselves in the local emergency room experiencing chest tightness and pain, shortness of breath and fearing a heart attack.

We use the terms grief, mourning and bereavement interchangeably, yet actually, they have different meanings. The word grief, derived from the Latin word *gravis*, means virulent and heavy. Think of your grief as the bucket containing every one of your emotions. Mourning is your expression of these emotions through your actions and reactions, such as crying, moaning and wearing black. The word bereavement is a derivative of an Old English word, which meant to rob or steal and in today's language, it represents a state of loss. In essence, you work your grief (in part) through mourning while in a state of bereavement.

You do not however work all of your grief through mourning, as most of your grief resolves only with the passage of time and by accepting your loss on a mental, physical and spiritual level. Contrary to the belief that we get over tragedies, we actually walk, and at times, stumble through them. Though we never recover totally, we eventually integrate our loss. Regardless of the paths we walk in our process of healing, ultimately, our experience becomes an essential part of who we are.

As evidenced by writings throughout history, grief, bereavement and mourning have always existed. However, we lacked the research and vocabulary for understanding the cycle of grief associated with death until 1969, when Dr. Elizabeth Kubler-Ross identified the five stages of dying based on her interviews with more than 500 dying patients.[24] This five-stage model included denial and isolation, anger, bargaining, depression and acceptance.[25] Some people reportedly experienced each stage in the outlined order, while others appeared to alter the order or pass over stages, avoiding them altogether.

Many hospice agencies circulate a handout based on this five stage model, entitled *The Grief Cycle.* Though variations exist, the basic structure includes a cycle of shock and denial, anger and guilt, bargaining, tears and fears, despair, depression and resignation, adjustment and acceptance and eventually healing. Originally, the final step was recovery, although later modified to either reconciliation, integration or healing.

This change was necessary as the word "recovery" implied that it was possible to return to your prior state of being. However, as you now know, you did not return to that prior place of innocence. In effect, experiencing the death of your companion has profoundly affected you.

During a grief group meeting, one of the widows concisely expressed her state of mind following her husband's sudden death. She said, "I lost him, and could not find me either." The sense of loss coupled with the sensation of being lost governs your emotions. Your world is out of focus and you have lost the ability to adjust your lens, to see or feel clearly. You are in a state of disorientation and sorrow because of the simultaneous death of your spouse, your identity as a mate, and your relationship.

Grief counselors advise that you will move through your grief at your own speed, sometimes avoiding, and other times finding yourself immersed in certain phases for extended periods. You will likely travel at varying speeds in forward and reverse motion in your journey towards healing and each time it will look and feel slightly different. Hold on to the knowledge that you are on your own path, grieving your own way and that no one has the right to deny you your grief or your grieving process, though many may try.

If your spouse died from an illness, he probably experienced his own unique stages of grief. Interestingly, those who die suddenly do not have time to work through these stages and perhaps die while in a state of shock, denial, or anger.[26] This concept presents a topic for consideration and dialogue with the remaining question being why some people get the opportunity for conscious awareness of their dying process while others die in a state of bewilderment.

There exists a school of thought that sudden death results in emotional anguish for the deceased because they do not have the opportunity to say their good byes, seek resolution or ask forgiveness. "And, like us who survive him, the person who died unexpectedly may be keenly aware of his unfinished business or regrets, which he feels helpless to communicate or resolve."[27]

If you accept this premise then continued dialogue with your deceased spouse is imperative. If unspoken issues remain, speak them now. If you believe it necessary and are capable of releasing him from any distressing emotional obligations, you may succeed in bringing both of you a measure of peace and comfort.

Apart from people's generalized inability to deal with grief, there exists a phenomenon known as disenfranchised grief. This means that for various reasons, society does not recognize a person's right and thus do not give him/her permission to grieve. Disenfranchised grief is a predicament that often occurs in same sex or non-married relationships and in deaths stemming from unpopular wars.

More subtle examples of where Americans sometimes disallow grief occur when the person's actions may have contributed to his own death such as a smoker dying from lung cancer, an alcoholic dying from liver disease or an overweight person dying of heart disease. If you follow this line of thinking, then we have no reason or right to grieve the death of a companion who had any unhealthy habits or disabilities. As a result, your love for this person becomes disenfranchised.

Public deaths that involve the media complicate coping and healing mechanisms. Examples of this would include the Oklahoma City bombing, the victims of the attacks on September 11 and space shuttle, mining or mountain climbing disasters. If your spouse's death propels you into the national spotlight, once the media takes over, grieving in normal fashion becomes problematic. Closure is also illusive when the death results in criminal or civil actions that remain alive in the courts for many years.

Other factors that complicate grief and healing include multiple deaths or losses, notoriety, an inability to recover the body, secrets discovered after or at the time of death and in situations when the body is not presentable.

Regardless of the scope of your loss, grief has many common elements. "Death embraces the personal, social, physical, and spiritual."[28] Earlier, I spoke of how the shock of losing your spouse affects you on each of these levels. A sense of vulnerability and irrational fear can overwhelm you for many months, even years. Your world, encased in that imagined snow globe comes to rest at a slant or upside down, awaiting the next upheaval.

Because of your vulnerability, you have an expectancy of more attacks on your stability. Regardless of prior or consecutive losses, this single experience profoundly and irrevocably changed you, and you are the only person who fully understands and recognizes your transformation. Your level of vulnerability will probably diminish. However, your heightened level of awareness will remain forever.

*"No one ever told me
that grief
felt so like fear"*

C.S. Lewis

Grief in Motion

The concept of grief in motion reflects the always changing, never knowing state of being wherein you now exist. Your grief comes in waves and you have no control over when or where the waves hit. The waves can knock you down or at least off balance. You will experience sneaker waves that catch you blindsided; seventh waves, reportedly the largest, (unfortunately you forgot to count, and are caught unaware) and tidal waves, the ones that knock you flat, pinning you under.

The anguish resulting from the death of your companion is often intense and brutal. Yet, our society allows us only a few months for a full recovery, and I call this the four-month rule. Four months represents that time when other people's patience with your grief meter expires. Amazingly, people think and suggest that you should be getting over your grief before you actually start grieving. Because sometimes the shock has to wear off before the grieving can begin.

It is crucial to remember that for the most part you physically look the same to other people. They cannot see your pain other than perhaps by the way you now slump a little or the anguish on your face. However, since your grief is not openly visible, for many people, it simply does not exist.

Grievers in their thirties and forties frequently report that their parents are pushing their recovery, and grievers in their fifties and sixties have their children suggesting that it is time to move on. If I were to venture a guess as to what perpetuates this need to fix us it would be that our family, friends and acquaintances may need assurance of their own quick mend, in the event they find themselves suffering a similar loss.

> *"In three words I can sum up everything*
> *I've learned about life: it goes on."*
>
> **Robert Frost**

Yes, life goes on however this statement and the concept are misleading, because it is a different life. It is a life you may not like and will probably not recognize. Adjusting to your new reality, your new normal, takes an inordinate amount of time. Initially, it is wise to minimize your expectations of what you can accomplish. Give yourself permission to change your mind and always have a back up plan or escape route. I found for many months following Joe's death that the kids and I would attend holiday or school functions, frequently leaving before the main event.

Occasionally, I anticipated the discomfort in advance. However, other events unexpectedly proved painful and at times produced feelings of claustrophobia and anxiety. My sons never argued with me about leaving so I assumed they felt uncomfortable as well. This lack of comfort, possibly rooted in the confusion of not knowing where we belonged, was unnerving. These were feelings that I had never before experienced but they were now a central part of my new found sense of insecurity.

Normalizing or feeling righted again takes a long time. As an analogy, picture the excessive amount of energy necessary to control a sailboat in storm driven seas. Eventually the wind dies down allowing the boat to right itself, yet during the storm righting the craft appeared hopeless or maybe just too difficult. Similarly, after each storm of grief passes, you find strength in the knowledge that you even survived and this awareness provides the impetus to try again the next day.

Strength is necessary because so many of the everyday activities become so very difficult, tasks that before required not much more than a thought or an activation of the subconscious. Now you often stand paralyzed, unable to grasp even the simplest of details, unable to complete even the basic tasks of daily living. This happens because your world has turned upside down and you have yet to find your new point of equilibrium.

This feeling is somewhat like standing on the shoreline when the tide goes out and you can feel the sand moving beneath your feet, pulling you off balance. You know you should seek out more solid ground, if only you knew where to find some. In the interim, your only hope is in maintaining your balance. All the while, everyone else you know walks by and with some pity, wonders if you are ever going to find your way out of the water.

A few months after Joe died, I wrote a note to my family and friends because I felt I needed to further explain what I was experiencing. From conversations with other widows, it appears that this need to explain is often necessary. My letter read in part,

> *"Joe died and I miss him terribly. I miss his touch, his laugh, his smile, his voice, and his presence. I miss him as my friend, my lover, my playmate, my co-parent, my past, my present, and my future. I cannot imagine my life without him in it. I now exist in a cloud of disorientation and despair. It feels as though I have a gaping hole in my stomach and my heart is shredded.*
>
> *There is no "fun" or "happy" in my emotional vocabulary. There are only days when I feel devastated; days when I feel sad; days when I feel anxious and angry, and every now and then, days when I feel okay. I spend my days trying to hold it all together. Trying to keep life as normal as possible for the kids, and trying to be there for them when they are sad. Sometimes they stroke my shoulders and crawl in to my lap so I can hold them while I cry.*
>
> *We have changed in a way that you cannot possibly understand and maybe in a way that is uncomfortable for all of you. Unfortunately, we cannot fix our broken hearts quickly, and we cannot expedite our recovery. Have patience with our healing process, for we have no idea how to get better."*

Associating with friends and family who are willing to let you, experience grief in your own way, at your own speed, is essential for your healing process.

"Courage does not always roar. Sometimes courage is the quiet voice at the end of the day saying, 'I will try again tomorrow'"

Mary Anne Radmacher

The First Hurdles

I spoke earlier of the fact that in every relationship one person customarily outlives the other. Yet, we do not really give thought to this reality at the beginning of our relationship. Outliving your companion is not an easy task and requires much adjustment; so it would make sense that we take some time to plan for this event. Unfortunately, because of the taboo surrounding death, we choose to ignore the inevitable; in essence, adopting an attitude of "hey, let's just wait and see what happens."

However, now that you have remained to pick up the pieces, it is imperative that you remember to eat, sleep and breathe. This reminder sounds basic and yet many of us in our grief forget. Even though I ate, my weight plummeted thirty pounds in eight weeks. Breathing happened sporadically, unevenly. I often found myself holding my breath (no, not holding it, just not breathing) unaware of what I was doing. Sleep presented many problems and at some juncture, I resorted to sleeping while the kids were in school because I was unable to sleep sufficiently at night.

As bedtime approached, my anxiety level increased markedly. I would lie on the bed, (which was no longer our bed - a harsh adjustment), stare at the ceiling and will my mind to shut down and my stomach to stop aching. Joe's suits and ties hung in the adjacent closet, just two feet away. His shoes lined the floor, polished, waiting. His new truck sat parked outside the bedroom window, another stark reminder of his sudden, unbelievable disappearance from our lives.

On the nights that I managed sleep, I frequently had nightmares and they were simply horrid. I would awaken in an emotional frenzy that for me capped off the misery of bedtime.

> *Anyone who has experienced the death of a loved one*
> *knows about that brief moment between when you awak-*
> *en and when you remember. As the moment passes, it hits*
> *you like a baseball bat to the head and stomach simulta-*
> *neously, often resulting in a loud moan or grimace and a*
> *strong desire to pull the pillow over your head in a feeble*
> *attempt to shut it back out.*

In my nightmares, Joe would tell me that he hated me and never wanted to see me again or he would mock me, saying that he was leaving me and I could do nothing to stop him. He laughed at my tears. He laughed as he walked away from me.

I remained stuck in that brief moment between awakening and remembering, while fully entrenched in the nightmare, before reality replaced my dreams, which was both different and worse. This punishing routine happened repeatedly, often many times a week and for several years.

In grief groups, no one spoke of a similar issue so I assumed that no one else experienced these types of nightmares. Then one day, I opened the book, *How to Survive the Loss of a Love*, and this passage made me feel less alone in my experience.

> "In my sleep I dreamed you called.
> You said you were moving back with your old lover.
> You said you thought a phone call would be the
> Cleanest way to handle it,
> "It" being that we could
> Never see each other again,
> And that I should understand why.
> I moved to wake myself and found
> I wasn't sleeping after all.
> My life became a nightmare."[29]

Another difficult task for the newly widowed involves dispensing of your husband or wife's clothes. Something in the back of your mind keeps telling you that if you give their clothes away they will have nothing to wear when they come back.

It was very disconcerting for me to discover Joe's clothes in the dryer after his funeral. Knowing that when I put his clothes into the dryer he was alive, yet by the time I retrieved them, he was dead. That just did not seem right.

Some of us pack up clothes within hours of hearing that our spouse has died. Others leave clothes in the closet and makeup on the vanity, for years. Some want help with this task and others do not. Whichever way you handle this is okay as there is no easy resolution. It is also okay to keep a few items even if you pack them away for a while. The clothes make memory bears, pillowcases or comforting quilts, for your kids or for you, to wrap around yourself on those especially long nights.

I recall suggesting that Joes' brother John and his cousin Frankie look through his suits, shirts, shoes and ties and take anything they wanted. They hesitated to take the nicer items, even though any remaining clothes would go to strangers. In effect, they also found themselves trapped in the belief that Joe would need his better clothes when he returned. Their reluctance to accept his death was evident, making the task too painful to complete.

> *This problem is the same for items specific to the deceased, such as tools, art supplies, scrapbooks, collector's items, etc. The difficulty with these items is that they now belong to no one. Even years later, you might feel a mix of sadness and disloyalty each time you stumble across this stuff or choose to give it away.*

The seemingly simple everyday task of grocery shopping can also prove arduous and at times unbearable. You walk down the aisles and reach for an item only he used, freezing midway as your brain registers the error. You pull back your hand, as if having touched a hot stove and look around to see if anyone noticed your mistake.

The issue is that food represents sustenance and denotes comfort and family. Food evokes strong sensory memories reminding us of that which no longer exists - that broken, irretrievable connection. As a result, there were occasions when I abandoned my cart and left the store, because continuing shopping made me sad or anxious. In response to this problem, I began minimizing my time in the store, only buying a few items each time. Eventually new shopping patterns emerged and the tendency to reach for the no longer needed item stopped.

There were also mornings when I would walk into the kitchen, still half asleep and reach into the cupboard for two coffee cups, not realizing what I was doing until the cups were in mid-air. I would feel the harshness of my new reality striking out at me and simultaneously obliterating my desire for coffee or anything else. On those mornings, I often wanted to return to bed, burrow under the covers and stay there until the pain receded. Instead, I would stand facing the shower, allowing the water to disguise my tears.

The newly widowed often find being out in public difficult. We find ourselves subjected to invariable public scrutiny, perception and interpretation. A woman whose husband had died the week before said that her co-workers seemed to be gauging her moods, all of them. If she felt sad and showed that emotion, they moved back, not wanting to share her space of grief. If she looked happy or laughed, they looked at her questioningly, perplexed by her ability to laugh. She felt trapped by their constant and endless appraisals.

I believe that these appraisals result from concern as well as from curiosity around what losing a spouse feels like. Occasionally, when this level of examination becomes overwhelming, it is necessary to get away from the observations and expectations of others.

It feels good when you can relax enough to stop checking your own responses and stop considering what others might be thinking about those responses. We actually experience some level of scrutiny in normal everyday life, but when consumed with grief, we may not have the energy to accommodate the inspection.

"Never apologize for showing feeling. When you do so, you apologize for the truth"

Benjamin Disraeli

The Split Personality of the Survivor

People vary regarding how much of their past, their opinions and their feelings they divulge to others, though generally women share more than their male counterparts do. I have always considered myself transparent, disclosing many of my life experiences, opting for an open book approach, seeing little or no advantage to keeping secrets. As such, I routinely struggle with understanding why people often conceal their true selves and by doing so present a false façade or a complete masque.

However, soon after Joe's death, I realized that other people's inability to deal with death and the ensuing grief, mandate that we mask the true depth of our grief and keep our emotional suffering to ourselves. The fact remains that most people are not prepared to comprehend or share in the extent of our pain.

As a result, I too erected a façade. I pretended that I was for the most part okay, even though I was more or less devastated. For the first time in my life, I understood what living a dual life felt like and I found it both convoluted and dishonest. Once my level of grief reached a livable plateau, the gap narrowed between my façade and my real self and seeing this progress may have accelerated my healing process.

The newly widowed suffer from something similar to an identity theft. Who you were yesterday you are no longer, yet you continue to lament over who and what you used to be. As a label, "Widow" is a potent word, implying a state of loss, sadness and the end of a relationship. You shift from saying we and ours to me and mine, a mindful and painful transition that does not occur easily. Every time you use the wrong pronoun, it is like receiving an electrical shock throughout your body, resulting in an involuntary jerk of your head. You are literally and figuratively shocked by your new identity, an identity defined only loosely by the word "widow".

One day at the local grocery store, I ran into a former employer. He started our conversation by saying, "Hey, are you still" and before he finished the sentence, I said, "No", because, no matter what his question was, "No" was the correct answer. I was not living in the same house, working at the same job, married to the same person or driving the same car. Everything had changed. I was experiencing a total identity theft because of the death of my spouse.

Amazingly, you have the choice of telling and retelling your story many times each day. With strangers, I would often take a moment to think about whether I had the energy for the truth because more often than not my mood or energy level dictated the nature of my response.

For example, on Father's Day or on Joe's birthday, we would go shopping for balloons or flowers and the clerk would smile at the kids and say, "Your dad is really going to like these." Sometimes, we would just nod and walk out. Other times one of the boys would look up and say, "He's dead", which of course resulted in an uncomfortable moment for the clerk.

I recall, with some bemused horror, sitting at a T ball game when another mom inquired how we were doing. For some reason, maybe because she looked like she really wanted to know, I just unloaded, telling her everything that was on my mind and in my heart at that moment. When I finished, approximately twenty minutes later, I could tell by the look on her face that I had shocked her beyond words. She mumbled something unintelligible in response, and actually ran away from me, stumbling in the process. I knew then that I had broken the expected code of silence, which was unacceptable, yet I had no regrets because being honest felt good.

Expression of grief is essential, making it imperative that widows express their grief through talking, writing or crying. Unexpressed thoughts have no voice and are thus incomplete, clouding our ability to understand our true feelings. Henry Wadsworth Longfellow eloquently stated, "Well has it been said that there is no grief like the grief which does not speak."

Verbalization allows the bereaved a feasible means of expressing their feelings, concerns and fears and this is why sharing your story every chance you get is helpful. Many people are not naturally inclined to write, though it is a viable avenue of expression and includes journaling, electronic mail and letter writing. Crying releases emotion in a more elemental and tangible fashion and provides a vital outlet. The avenue of communication you choose doesn't matter as long as you don't choose silence.

"I measure every grief I meet
with narrow probing eyes.
I wonder if it weighs like mine
or has an easier size."

Emily Dickinson

Secondary Losses

Many factors help determine the level of grief incurred in widowhood and several of them can encumber the healing process. The manner of death is usually significant. However, it is also necessary to realize that the death is the primary loss. The secondary losses encompass everything else that occurs as the result of that death.

Often the secondary losses are many and considerable and can include housing, money, structure, and the loss of friends, social activities, identity and a sense of security. The primary and secondary losses interact and combine to comprise your overall loss.

The determining factors include, but are probably not limited to, the strength and basis of your relationship, your available support systems, the role of your spouse within the family structure, the existence of children and their stage of development, financial security, personal health, religious and cultural framework, concurrent losses and your level of resiliency.

Resiliency involves a person's ability to cope with adverse situations. If you take time to observe others, you will realize that everyone manages stress and loss differently A significant problem or crisis to one person is often not an issue to another. As with issues of grief, levels of resiliency vary for each individual.

Literature defines resiliency as either a characteristic of the person, a characteristic of the environment, or an outcome of prior experience.[30] In essence, experiencing prior losses can enhance one's level of resiliency.

The strength, duration and dynamics of your relationship will influence both your grief and ultimately your healing process. What role did your spouse play in your relationship?

What were his household responsibilities within the family? Did you share the same hobbies and activities? Was he your sole provider of everything, some things or nothing?

Your employment or financial status is also significant. Can you financially survive without your husband's income or pension? Are you eligible for social security? What is your job training or education? Have you worked outside the home ever or in the past twenty years? Do you have life insurance, savings or accessible retirement monies? How much are your adjusted finances going to affect your lifestyle and choices?

Having minor children is another crucial factor that influences your capacity to cope with your loss. Their ages and stage of development ultimately affect their ability to comprehend their loss. You now have sole responsibility for their normal everyday needs coupled with their grieving process. Because you are a parent, their grief becomes your grief.

If they are young, you may have to find childcare to fill the gap left by your spouse's death. People often do not appreciate or realize the difference between solo parenting and two-parent households or even parents who live in separate houses but remain actively involved in their children's lives. It is not just about the daily stressors. If you need to attend evening meetings or run errands, you can no longer divide and conquer. Everywhere you go twenty-four hours a day, seven days a week, you have to either take all of your children with you or find an alternative resource.

Obviously, this is more of an issue for widowed parents with children under the age of twelve. In addition, if you are the sole wage earner and your spouse handled the majority of childcare, this presents an even bigger obstacle in reconstructing your spouse's role within the family.

The presence of a support network of family, friends and members of your community can greatly influence your ability to adjust to your new normal. In addition to daily living activities, having people support you in your grief is immeasurable. Conversely, the absence of this is arduous.

This is the time in your life when support is necessary and where significant friendships can emerge. If you have no one in your circle of friends and family who can relate to your loss, you need to seek out other widow's or a grief support group.

If you are in poor health then the added stress will undoubtedly exacerbate your illness. Many physical ailments accompany grief, regardless of your awareness of their presence. You have most likely neglected self and professional care. However, it is imperative at this point in your life, that you take the best possible care of yourself. It is equally important that you set reachable goals, have flexible expectations of yourself and if possible maintain a sense of humor.

The manner in which your spouse died is also germane. This has been evident in my discussions with and observations of other widows. The varying causes of death included accidents, homicide, suicide, medical malpractice, short lived or prolonged illness, and sudden death from a health-related issue.

Comparing the grief experience in having your spouse die suddenly rather than following a prolonged illness is difficult to assess because of a multitude of complexities. "It is impossible to measure the torment incurred by sudden death against the drawn out agony of a slow death… the circumstances of death were always particular to an individual, as were the responses of those who grieved for them."[31] I have participated in many discussions about whether anticipated or unanticipated death is more difficult. At the end of these conversations, everyone usually agrees that both are miserable and neither is uncomplicated.

However, unanticipated death frequently results in a more severe grief reaction than one would experience in an anticipated death. This occurs for several reasons, including the fact that the sudden death is often violent in nature. "The effect of a sudden death is considered so devastating that it has been coined the 'unexpected loss syndrome.'"[32]

When widowed as the result of an unexpected death, we struggle with accepting the death, the avalanche of emotions and our lack of preparation. "The survivor is thrown immediately into a world of uncertainty and unknowns. A sudden death is an assault on one's sense of power and orderliness. Suddenly nothing seems sacred, safe or secure."[33] Especially oneself…if they can go that easily…well, you now realize that you and everyone else you know and love are susceptible to the same fate.

Deaths resulting from suicide, homicide or accidents carry additional burdens. Survivors often harbor feelings of self-blame or they blame the deceased or a third party. The endless "what if's" and "but for's" can convolute the survivors anxiety and sorrow and thus add to their level of grief.

Occasionally the spouse's remains are not presentable or not recoverable. How this affects the survivors often depends on their religious and cultural framework. I could hardly imagine the tribulations connected with having your spouse disappear and presumed dead with no concrete understanding of what happened to him.

"Grieving is world-oriented, and those who have entered into this deep emotion are expressing what we all feel and are afraid to face."

Robert Sardello

Friends and Family: How They Can Hurt & How They Can Help

The death of your spouse often parlays into the potential for losing friends; friends who are incapable of continuing your relationship with them once you lose your couple status and friends who simply cannot deal with your grief and loss. However, because of your loss, you may also experience the emergence of new and significant friendships.

It is a normal to have expectations of others and widows often struggle with the things that do not happen, with the people who walk away instead of staying on to help. My feeling is that if you expect another to do something and he or she does not fulfill your expectation, you will always remember their lack of response because of your level of disappointment. Conversely, if someone does something beyond what you expected, then you will always remember that response because their actions exceeded your expectations.

The purpose of this section is to share common experiences as well as some possible explanations for the why people inadequately cope with grief and loss. Some widows may believe that their friends and family members exceeded, or at least met, all of their expectations. However, we usually hear more about the disappointments.

How they can hurt:

In general, people do not know how to help friends in grief. The newly widowed frequently report feeling abandoned by friends and family especially those directly connected to the deceased. I witnessed this countless times in grief groups, and in the aftermath of my husband's death and during my family's experience at Bridges. Bridges is a Center for Grieving Children, located in Tacoma, Washington. The widowed parents, who met separately, all shared stories about their families, co-workers and friends' inability to communicate with them during or after the death of their spouses.

> *Some of their stories were humorous and some shock-ing, but most were sad. They spoke of new friendships and bonds, but ultimately they wanted to talk about the relationships that failed to survive their experience with death, which was attributed to an overall inability to talk about death and dying. The truth is that some people just do not feel comfortable around this depth of grief and oth-ers struggle with not knowing how to help.*

People in grief often talk about the clichés they hear throughout their grieving process. It would be of great benefit if we could distribute "proper speak" pamphlets to friends, family and co-workers in times of sorrow. Unfortunately, there are no such pamphlets readily available, and in an honest yet futile attempt to communicate (and in hoping to ease the sorrow), the clichés spill out.

My most mind-boggling example went like this: On the Monday following Joe's death I was at school picking up the boys. One of their friend's fathers came over and said, "I'm sorry about your loss." He then pointed at me and added rather loudly, "It could have been worse." He walked off without my responding and I never knew what he meant, (he probably didn't know either). If nothing else, this example provided a good anecdote for many years, especially when speaking with the be-reaved about their interpretation of what others say to them.

Some of the most frequently spoken clichés are *Don't worry, you'll meet someone new; You'll get over this in time; God wanted him in heaven; He's in a better place;* and my least favorite, which we heard repeatedly, *At least he died doing something fun* or *At least he died happy.* Perhaps I am unique here, however I am certain that I did not feel any better because Joe died having fun and I am equally certain that Mike and Nick didn't either. It is conceivable that this component might make a difference in situations where no children are involved.

Perhaps this fun factor helps alleviate the grief of people who are not that close to the deceased; however, I question whether it helps many of the close friends or immediate family members. To this date, when I look at the pictures of Joe playing in the snow on the day he died, it only makes me sad, sad that he erred in judgment that day and sad that he died.

Having said that, other widows may find comfort in knowing their spouses died doing something fun. I will agree that dying happy trumps dying unhappy. Aside from violent death, many sudden deaths occur while we are engaged in a recreational activity, at work or while driving, and I would assume that most are happy in those endeavors. It is also possible that age is crucial in the fun factor element. If your spouse died enjoying his favorite pastime at the age of eighty, dying doing something he loved probably makes a difference.

The bottom line is that people frequently stumble badly when trying to express their condolences, when the best thing they could say is as simple as, *It's good to see you; How can I help;* or *I'm sorry that your husband died.* Regardless of what they say, it helps to remember that their intent is usually well meaning.

Many widows have expressed some ire and a sense of defensiveness when someone says to them, *you are doing so well - you must be very strong.* This bothers them because on the contrary, they feel that they are not doing well at all but remain in a constant struggle to regain some sense of normalcy, an exhausting and unending effort.

As such, they do not appreciate receiving a compliment on what is in essence their acting ability and feel that these comments veil the difficulty of their daily battle. It also illustrates other people's inability to comprehend the depth of grief experienced in the death of a companion. Contrary to this position, one widow stated that she felt encouraged by a similar statement because she was not sure how she was doing and this statement empowered her.

Another approach taken by friends and family is to stop talking about the deceased as if he or she never existed. Many widows have shared stories of relatives and friends who deleted the deceased from their conversations. I similarly experienced a friend talking about a vacation we took the year before Joe died.

He kept talking about the trip that Nick, Mike and I took omitting Joe from the memory. At first, I thought I was confused or going crazy (again), thinking that maybe I had the dates mixed up. Then I realized that he was rewriting history and leaving Joe out on purpose. I am not sure if he felt this was helpful or if he simply found it too difficult to include Joe in his story. Regrettably, regardless of his reasoning, leaving him out didn't help me.

A woman widowed twenty years ago shared that her late husband's friends were shocked when she remarried. She guessed that these friends thought she should stay single, out of respect or something else to which she was not privy. After pausing, she added that these friends were never around at 2:00 in the morning to help her when the kids cried out in the middle of the night, sick or startled by nightmares, or in missing their dad. Nor did they help pay the bills, mow the lawn or take care of her. Nearly two decades after the death of her husband, she still harbored bad feelings about the lack of understanding and support and she still grieved for the end of their friendship.

Criticizing or judging the newly widowed is neither beneficial nor productive. However, widows frequently report that friends and family critically assess the decisions they make. Many widows contend that others have no right to judge without having experienced a similar loss. William Shakespeare said, "Everyone can master a grief but he that has it."

In other words, everyone thinks that he or she knows better what is best for those who are grieving. Examples of these criticisms include decisions regarding finances, school changes, selling the house or moving, kid's bedtimes, discarded holiday traditions, cemetery visits, movie choices, dating and so forth.

Family and friends often fail to grasp that just getting out of bed each morning takes nearly every ounce of energy, and as a result the once adhered to family schedule changes. Nothing of the former life remains the same, some adjustments are slight and some are monumental.

Ralph Waldo Emerson captured this revised reality when he said, "Death puts life into perspective." Family decisions are now a product of this renewed sense of perspective coupled with an extreme shortage of energy caused by the combination of your grief and having to take on your spouse's roles within the household.

You may encounter friends and family members who forever remain uncomfortable, distant or aloof in the presence of your grief. Many people in grief groups report similar circumstances and state that they struggle with understanding and accepting this lack of support. It would help if we could put out a sign that reads, "Help wanted, just hang around for awhile and see what needs to be done." Even for those individuals who cannot stand too close fearing that the grief will engulf them, there is always something they can do, out there on the perimeter.

Customarily widows' resist asking for help and this resistance stems from their overwhelming needs. It is more difficult to decipher what someone can do for you when your to do list is endless. It works best if others can identify ways they can help you, tasks like mowing the lawn, taking out the garbage, household repairs, hanging the Christmas lights, delivering food, house cleaning, picking up groceries, pulling weeds, or taking the kids to ballgames or the park.

Unfortunately, there are those people in our lives who cannot actively participate in any manner other than by expressing frustration and at times boredom with our grieving process. I believe that this arises solely from their not having experienced a significant loss or sometimes from their lack of compassion. They remain in a state of unawareness or ignorance, a state that because of your loss, you have now transcended. You cannot change them. However, you can choose to either change your expectations of them or end your relationship.

Regrettably, upon hearing of a death in the community, friends postpone visits with surviving family members, often until the receiving line following the funeral service. They suffer the "*dis-ease*" of being in close proximity with death and grief. They rationalize this delay by believing that family members need privacy and would thus find visits and phone calls intrusive or bothersome. On the contrary, I contend that it is good for friends to call the bereaved and at least give them the option of your company.

On a positive note, because of your experience and your survival, you are a gift to every one you know, now and forever: you will support them in their grief and you won't question their healing schedule. Reaching out to an-

other person who has incurred a loss through death can help both of you. They will benefit from your ability to empathize and you will benefit from your ability to help.

As is customary, it does not take long for support to wane as people return to their daily lives and time marches onward. Their loss was not as acute; his presence in their lives not as absolute, and thus it was easier for them to adjust to his absence. Some widows are fortunate to have large families who live near and are available for as long as needed. However, I think it is more common for widows to be left primarily on their own, assimilating their loss and often struggling with their healing process.

How they help:

Not everyone voices negative opinions about your grieving process or your decisions. Some widows find themselves in the fortunate situation of being surrounded by friends and family who are incredibly supportive and truly helpful. They simply take over until you are ready and able to resume your role at work or in the family.

In our situation, friends, family and members of the community offered support, companionship and thoughtfulness. A few people exceeded any possible expectations. Suzanne, whose son Chris was Mike's friend, provided a formidable example of what help can look like. Even though I knew her before Joe died, we were not close friends. However, the day after he died she came over and sat at the dining room table, wide eyed and stunned. She had no idea what to do; yet, she sat there watching, waiting and available.

She did this day after day and eventually the density of grief in the house became less frightening for her. I am not certain why she stayed to help, only that her help was immeasurable. Frequently, she would drop her oldest son off to child sit, and take me out for dinner or a movie. Other times, she would take the kids and give me a much-needed break. Her kindness continued for years and we soon became close friends.

Jim, another parent of one of Mike's friends, also surprised me with his level of generosity. On multiple occasions, he took the boys to parks, games, concerts and helped install playground equipment in our yard.

In his efforts, he actually returned some of the normal-ness to Mike and Nick's world. His wife Anne sent us a card every month for the first year just to say they had not forgotten.

As stated earlier, unexpected compassion often has more of an impact simply by its having been unanticipated. Both Suzanne and Jim displayed a level of compassion that continued for many months.

Some of my best grief therapy occurred while taking frequent walks with my new friend, Debbie. Her husband died from cancer the year after Joe. She was raising three children, all in grade school. We walked the waterfront, two miles each way, as fast as we could. We talked and we laughed. We laughed about things that no one else would find funny. We talked about everything and anything. Nothing was taboo. We belonged to the secret society of widows with knowledge acquired by profound loss, recognized only by other members. We found healing and safe harbor in each other's company.

Our family was entrenched in the St. Patrick's School and Parish community, meaning we were ensconced in a safety net of sorts. Everywhere we went, church, school, baseball, cub scouts, the grocery store, everyone knew our story, which also meant that everyone knew and spoke of how we were progressing and how well we were surviving our loss. Some of this attention stemmed from curiosity, because no one really knows how he or she would handle a similar tragedy. Yet there was no shortage of compassion.

I recall the sympathetic looks, especially on holidays, which is when I realized that they had no way of knowing that today was not really any worse than yesterday or any easier than tomorrow. Only those who walked the same path understood the drama presented by each day, a drama not just reserved for holidays. Throughout all of this, I maintained a faith that we were going to survive our loss and that somehow we would emerge stronger.

After church one Sunday, I spoke with a man whose wife died in a car accident leaving him to raise their four young children. I expressed frustration in the staleness of my healing process. Even though we were standing side by side, he continued to look straight ahead and said, "Don't worry, you have the rest of your life to get over this." I only nodded, offering no verbal response. His comment may have seemed peculiar to the people around us, but I understood his meaning as this: That adjusting to our loss was not something we could rush and that peace would come in time. At the same time, he knew, and I was learning, that no matter how long we lived; the pain associated with the memory of our loss would always remain.

Fortunately, I was also discovering that once fully absorbed, we would acknowledge our loss differently. For at least the first year, I wore my widowhood in front of me. I viewed myself as a widow first and everything else was secondary. In some well-deserved state of pity, I also thought of myself as a new member of a club for which I never sought membership and it seemed unfair that I was suffering so much because of a choice someone else made.

Then somewhere I heard that it is better if you allow your experience to refine you, and not define you. This perspective helped me understand that I would find greater peace in stepping through the veil of widowhood, than I would find by letting it settle over me. At this point in my grief process, a metamorphosis occurred and I shifted from victim to survivor, from not caring if I died, to being okay with living.

In-laws

> *Visiting with in-laws once the connecting family member has died is an entirely new and at times complicated event. There exists a sense of not fitting in, like a puzzle with strategic pieces missing. Some people transcend the resulting quandary and others do not. Some manage to overlap the missing pieces, while others never reconnect. In my opinion, the ability to reconstruct the relationship is most significant for the children. It is important that half their family does not disappear with the death of one parent.*

Joe's mom was unquestionably heartbroken over his death. She saved all of the bereavement cards, unopened, for our first visit. She saved the Christmas presents Joe and I had purchased together, also unopened, initially because of her sister's illness, then because of Joe's death.

On arrival, her eyes met mine and we connected in grief, a grief that was different in nature, yet similar in depth. We could sit together in understanding, linked by our loss. Still, the pervasiveness of Joe's absence forced everyone to explore his or her new roles in our relationship.

The frequency of our summer trips to visit Joe's family in New Jersey has declined and they have not visited since I remarried. This decline may stem from busy schedules and a lack of planning or they may feel tentative or uncomfortable, not knowing how they would fit in to our newly constructed family. Regardless, preserving the family connection is vital for the children's sake.

"That the dead stay dead is a constant surprise"

Author Unknown

Depression and Anxiety

Early on in my grief, I read the aforementioned quote and it resonated with me on some very deep level. How many times I found myself in a state of forgetfulness or unaware, wherein I needed reminding that not only was Joe dead, but that he would remain dead forever. How many times did I think he would walk through that door or up those stairs? On some level, I believed that his death would not last, that somehow, he would come back to us, and there were times when I sat and waited or searched for him in the crowd. Of course, he never came back.

Before Joe's death, I had never experienced death up close and personal. How can someone so alive one moment be so dead the next? Why did I not know that death meant gone, totally and forever? Can anyone really understand the permanency of death without experiencing a direct and pertinent loss?

My grandparents died in their seventies and eighties and though I missed them, I did not find their deaths disturbing. I thought of their deaths simply as a natural progression of their lives. Obviously, my husband's death was quite different because of his age and the unexpectedness of his death. In truth, I was entirely unprepared for the detour my life took that day.

Prior to his death I never experienced any level of anxiety or depression. However, subsequently I became accustomed to frequent attacks of anxiety and bouts of depression. They arrived without warning and seemingly without added reason. At times, they were severe enough that I struggled to breathe and I felt like someone was jumping up and down on my chest. Other times, a wave of depression would crash over me without warning, both of which made me want to scream and run away; and sometimes I did, but never far.

The kids needed a ride home from school.

"I found in you a home. Your departure left me a Shelter less victim of a Major Disaster. I called the Red Cross, but they refused to send over a nurse"[34]

The depression and anxiety I experienced after Joe died was tangible. It stayed with me for the better part of two years. There is much research and dispute about the use of prescription medications for situational depression. (Since I had never experienced depression before, Joe's death was considered a situation that caused my depression). In my case, the anti-anxiety medication, though taken rarely, was necessary. I also believe that the anti depression medication helped.

I have heard that some doctors will not prescribe anti depressants or anti anxiety medications, because they feel that the newly widowed need to experience their grief un-medicated. I concur that grief has to be experienced. However, because there are so many variables, I am hopeful that doctors will avoid painting all of us with the same brush, and realize that for some people medication is germane to their healing process.

Many people in grief believe that they lost ground after several months. This is usually not accurate though we often forget the pain that was. During these occurrences, if you take a moment and reflect back to the time immediately following your loss, you will undoubtedly recall that every moment of every day was awful; and now, only some moments of some days are awful.

We refer to these awful moments as "Grief bursts" where seemingly out of nowhere, the grief strikes in relentless fashion. You had stabilized for a time and now feel that you are slipping back into the void. "Grief comes in unexpected surges, mysterious cues set off a reminder of grief. It comes crashing like a wave, sweeping me in its crest, twisting me inside out…then recedes."[35] Though difficult, it is helpful if you can remember that this burst of grief will pass and you will emerge from it stronger than before. Most agree that you never fall back quite as far and that you surface slightly ahead of where you were the last time.

Like grief, the healing process varies from one individual to another and for many reasons. What matters to you is that however long it takes you is acceptable. You and your relationship are unique and this uniqueness precludes a standard healing process. Some widows complete their grieving in a matter of months and others never transcend their loss. Most people reach a level of reconciliation somewhere in between.

Life in our house remained upside down for many, many months. In retrospect, I recall that it took twelve months before I felt even remotely better and eighteen months to reach a level of existence where I felt we would probably survive our loss. After two years, I finally grasped the permanency of Joe's death, meaning I knew that he was not coming back. Somewhere between the fourth and fifth anniversary of his death, I was finally able to recall the good times, envision him laughing and gradually began remembering the love we shared.

Mike and Nick's grief journey seemingly followed a similar path. Though we talked about Joe constantly, it took five years for them to watch home movies and look through family photographs. Even though I offered, they have not wanted to visit the place where their father died. Perhaps they never will.

"It's not the wound that shapes our lives; it's the choices we make as adults between embracing our wounds or raging against them."

Geneen Roth

Not everyone struggles with forgiving his or her deceased spouse, either because forgiveness is not an issue or because it is not an obstacle. Unfortunately, it was a significant issue and an unyielding obstacle for me. Forgiving Joe for dying the way he did proved elusive because I did not understand the choices he made that day. Maybe if we had been childless it would have been different, but it was terribly hard watching our sons struggle day after day with the fact that their dad was dead.

I recall receiving a summons from two of Mike's 3rd grade teachers on the same day. They reported that he appeared shut down, uninvolved, lethargic and thus not doing well in his classes, which obviously caused them concern. We were fourteen months out from the date of Joe's death and both boys had gone through many months of counseling. Nearly every day we consciously processed our loss and yet on that day, it felt as though we were swimming against the tide.

I bring this up because it was a specific day wherein I recall being extremely angry with Joe for dying. I do not honestly think that in my entire life I had ever been so angry. I drew a direct connection between the choices Joe made and Mike's struggle on that day and my anger was overwhelming.

Part of my dilemma with comprehending his death was that I did not possess an ounce of desire to participate in recreational risk taking or any form of reckless behavior. As a result, I struggled with forgiving Joe for how he died. To me, it seemed an amazingly stupid way to die. My male friends and relatives have told me that they do not consider riding snowmobiles a risk and I can agree with that premise if we remove alcohol and speed from the equation.

They have tried unsuccessfully to enlighten me regarding the innate relationship between men and risk taking behavior, which I ultimately deem an inherent difference between males and females and thus feel incapable of understanding.

I believe that becoming a parent equates with making responsible choices. In essence, I felt that having children at home should have influenced Joe's behavior and because it apparently didn't, I was angry. Regrettably, I realized that my unresolved anger, my inability to forgive him, complicated my healing process. Yet it took many years for me to reach a point where, though I would never understand his choices, I could at least forgive him.

"There is no pain so great as the memory of joy in present grief"

Aeschylus

Holidays Revised

You have heard that the first year of holidays and celebrations is the hardest and I agree. The second year is not exactly a breeze but definitely easier. Having a plan in place well ahead of the date is the best preparation. In order to get through these firsts, it is crucial that you do whatever makes you feel good. It is a time to think of your survival, not of other people's expectations and feelings.

This is new and often frightening territory for you. Give yourself permission to reinvent the holidays, at least for the first year. Remember that whatever emotions you experience are acceptable. Deciding to leave the Christmas decorations in storage, opting out of decorating a tree, declining invitations to annual events are only a few examples of the many activities you can revise.

Be reasonable, be flexible and be mindful of your possible need to escape. Try not to trap yourself into an across town dinner without a way to get home in case your emotions get the best of you. Elect or appoint yourself queen or king for the holidays and choose what makes you feel best. Give yourself permission to change your mind, all the while remembering that each of these holidays is only 24 hours long.

You may need to let go of some treasured traditions and you will undoubtedly create new ones. If you have children, it is crucial to include them in these decisions. Explain to them why some traditions cannot continue and then get their input about new customs, including those honoring their deceased mother or father.

Try having this discussion well in advance of the holiday season. Make a list of things you did in the past, including baking, cooking, gifts, decorating, cards, parties etc., and then decide which ones you can live without, especially the first year.

There are many personal ways to honor the deceased. Some families light candles, set a place at the table, share memories or have a small graveside ceremony. A favorite event with children involves writing notes to their deceased parent and inserting the notes inside balloons for the kids to set free.

Creating a memory table, making special ornaments, having everyone sign and decorate a holiday tablecloth, buying gifts or food for the less fortunate or planting a tree in memory of your loved one are some projects that have helped families through the holidays. In one of his grief seminars, Doug Smith suggested that each family member consider what he or she is most thankful for having received from the deceased. They write it down, put the paper in a box and place it under the tree. As each member of the family reads aloud what they wrote, the spirit of gift giving continues.

During holidays, others may criticize the decisions you make, especially if you are opting out of a family gathering. Keep in mind that without having experienced similar circumstances, they have a difficult time understanding your choices. I recall hearing that someone voiced concern over our choosing a movie and dinner out on our first Thanksgiving. They felt that this choice was potentially damaging for Mike and Nick because they needed tradition.

The first problem with maintaining our tradition was that Joe cooked all of our meals. Secondly, five and eight year old boys are not particularly fans of turkey, dressing, mashed potatoes and yams. Lastly, preparing a Thanksgiving feast for one adult and two children lacked appeal, at least for me. As a family, we decided how we wanted to celebrate the holiday and never regretted our choice.

Many of our holiday customs required tweaking. Joe went crazy over Halloween, turning our partially completed basement into an annual haunted house. Unfortunately, after his death, most of these decorations seemed morbid so I gave them away, which meant the end of our haunted house as well as the majority of our decorations.

At Christmas, he spent days stringing outdoor and indoor lights. We baked, shopped, cooked, entertained, and celebrated. He prepared cheesecakes as well as exotic meals for each of the holiday dinners. Fortunately, I could bake cookies, shop and cook basic meals; however, stringing outdoor lights and preparing exotic dinners were no longer a part of our family tradition. Chopping down a tree and getting it into the stand was not in my realm of possibilities either. Instead, we selected a decent fake tree. This decision helped not only initially but also in the years that followed.

Traditionally, we hung stockings for each of us and Santa would fill them with little treasures on Christmas Eve. In preparation for our first year, we sat and talked about whether or not to hang Joe's stocking. Mike and Nick decided that we should, and I felt good about our decision making process.

Then I overheard Nick as he walked away saying, "I wonder what Santa will bring dad this year" and then I realized that I now had to fill the stocking. Buying stocking stuffers for my deceased spouse was not at all therapeutic. After standing in the middle of the mall for a very long time, sad and confused, I finally purchased household items, such as batteries, film and a small flashlight.

Holidays inevitably look different following the death of your spouse. A curse of widowhood includes the tendency and ability to recollect every detail of the prior year's celebration, with added speculation as to how you might have done things differently had you known it would be your last one together. Throughout these days, I found myself comparing each holiday to the prior year, committing the images to memory in fear of forgetting.

Deciding what changes your family can live with helps when navigating the various holidays. Remember that two-parent households struggle with all of the holiday expectations, without the grief component, so give yourself a break when choosing what you alone can accomplish.

"*My grief lies all within,
and these external manners
of laments are merely
shadows to the unseen grief
that swells with silence
in the tortured soul*"

William Shakespeare

"Complicated" Grief

I hesitated to add this section because there is much professional debate about the diagnosis as well as the definition of complicated grief, a term that is perhaps over used in grief literature and often misinterpreted by people suffering from grief as well as their families and friends.

Historically, psychologists generalized the grieving process in terms of psychological stages necessary in recovering from a loss.[36] Regrettably, not everyone traverses these stages of grief successfully. Approximately 10% to 20% of those surviving the death of a loved one suffer from a condition known as "complicated grief" requiring professional intervention.[37]

For many months, these individuals endure intense and persistent symptoms, including distress, disbelief, anger, separation and loneliness and are incapable of assimilating their loss into their construction of reality.[38]

Complicated grief includes an inability to reconstruct a meaningful personal reality, and insecure individuals struggling with their sense of self and their relationships to others are especially vulnerable.[39] "Although the psychosocial accommodation to any death is significant, bereavement that is traumatic in nature...or that which violates the 'natural order'... poses additional challenges to the survivor's adaptation."[40] Violating the natural order occurs with the death of a child, an unexpected and sudden death, or when a person dies before their parents or elder siblings.

In suffering a complicated grief, some of the widowed
remain frozen in place. They endure intense and persistent
symptoms and actions, including giving away possessions,
entertaining thoughts of suicide, refusing to acknowledge
the death, paranoid reactions, withdrawal from friends
and family, flat affect, hallucinations, severe anger or guilt
and a generalized inability to cope with their loss.

Often well meaning friends and family members believe you are not reconciling quite quickly enough and suggest you have a more serious problem when in truth you are grieving in a normal fashion.

During a grief group, a woman widowed ten months prior, whose husband died unexpectedly, shared with the others how she handled her children's excessive concern with her healing process. She asked that they give her one year and if they did not notice an improvement during that time, she would see a specialist. They retreated, observed and reported within months that they in fact noticed her progress.

I would ask that you consider this story when thinking that you or someone else suffers from complicated grief. If you can see progress, then your healing process is likely on track.

Keep in mind that looking back in regret results in your inability to move forward. If while driving down the road you remained focused on the scene in your rear view mirror, you would certainly crash. There is nothing wrong with acknowledging your loss as long as you attend to today and by doing so take care of tomorrow in the process. "Healing is not forcing the sun to shine, but letting go of that which blocks the light."[41] It is important for you to see a grief counselor, your physician or at least attend a grief support group if you are questioning your ability to move forward.

*"Grief knits two hearts
in closer bonds than
happiness ever can;
and common sufferings
are far stronger links
than common joys."*

Alphonse De Lamartine

Grief Support Groups

The group forum offers a safe and appropriately structured environment for grieving. In conversing with others, you can better understand and validate your feelings and reactions and this will help you to gain perspective about surviving your loss. "Although not every person going through a bereavement process needs professional intervention, everyone needs support and social contact as they deal with the frightening aspects of grief…Social support can help rebuild the person again."[42]

> *Contrary to popular belief, grief support groups are not depressing. They provide you with a network of people who know what you are going through. This process allows you to normalize your grief, ultimately helping you to understand that you are not alone and are not going crazy. There are some tears, there is much laughter and both serve to help you heal.*

Many people have little or no association with community support systems and therefore lack the knowledge of how to access them when necessary. "In loosely knit networks, because the social system is not affected significantly, there are no rituals for rehabilitation of survivors and consequently, the individual receives very little social support"[43]

The intrinsic value of available support systems depends in part on the surviving individuals' perception of the support they are receiving from friends, relatives, civic and social groups. Several years ago a woman in a grief group stated that she had no support, when in actuality many members of her church community were helping her with yard work, cooking, cleaning, errands etc. Once someone questioned her about her perception of support, we learned that she was referring to the fact that her children were not helping her, which to her translated to no support.

Support networks have collapsed because of the trend in this country wherein people seldom identify with others outside of their family. This is especially true for the retired and elderly, though many of us no longer associate with or even know our neighbors.

Conversely, in pre-industrial society, death was within the community and therefore disrupted the social structure, resulting in both the family and the community grieving together.[44] In other words, everyone in the community understood and experienced your loss. As a result, they were often more supportive and less likely to dismiss your grief. Society consisted of interwoven structures as opposed to individual segments. When a husband and father died, the widow and children had to accept assistance from the community in order to survive.

The safety, freedom, and understanding that Debbie and I experienced on our walks resonated with the success of grief groups. Even if you have well-meaning friends who will let you say or do anything, only someone who has experienced a similar loss can even begin to appreciate your reality.

The death of a loved one, whether sudden or prolonged, encompasses a multitude of emotions and issues for surviving family members. Bereavement support for spouses and children is paramount and even more potentially significant when the loved one dies prematurely and unexpectedly. In these situations, many survivors experience shock and separation anxiety because they had insufficient time to prepare themselves for their loss.[45]

Following Joe's death, the kids and I attended grief group meetings at Bridges, a Center for Grieving Children, in Tacoma, WA. Its motto at that time was, "So that no child will grieve alone." They are an affiliate of Mary Bridge Children's Hospital and Health Center. Their program runs September through May with a summer retreat. The focus of the program is on the children; however, they also offer support groups for the accompanying adults.

The Bridges program facilitators designate different meetings for children whose parents or siblings died from violence versus accident or illness. The center further divided the surviving spouses by their experiences of anticipated versus unanticipated deaths. In separating these groups, the Bridges program lends validity to the premise that the grief recovery process may differ depending on the nature of the loss and as such, the participants would benefit most by meeting with others who suffered similar losses.[46]

In addressing grief and bereavement, community and non-profit organizations such as hospice agencies, churches/temples, funeral homes, hospitals and community centers provide us the opportunities to attend grief group meetings as well as seminars on preparing for holidays. Many of these organizations also distribute brochures pertinent to grief resolution, in hope that we will have a better understanding of our grief as a normal healing process.

Gaining validation of your grief experience is crucial to your healing. When you need to talk about your loss or your grief and everyone else seems annoyed or inconvenienced, a grief group or another individual who has experienced a similar loss, provides you with a safe place, a necessary place

"The presence of her absence is everywhere"

Edna S. Vincent Millay

Men & Grief

I am hopeful that men reading this section of the book do not find only these pages applicable. There are many commonalities amongst grievers that transcend diversities, including gender. Having stated this, there also exist some distinct differences between men and women in how they experience grief.

Author, speaker and grief educator, Doug Smith, talks about women as intuitive grievers and men as instrumental grievers. He explains that men, in general, work their grief physically instead of emotionally. Grieving males benefit from physical exertion through exercise or hard labor. The garage, shop, or yard provides a safe haven of healing. In my experience, this concept has proven to be consistently reliable and has often provided restorative insight.

Men are also reportedly better at compartmentalizing their grief. As their emotions surface, they acknowledge them and then cognitively set them aside to be dealt with later. I have heard many men say something like, "Of course I'm sad, but when I'm at work, I just don't think about what happened." In essence, men are capable of separating their emotions from their behaviors, a feat that most women would find unachievable as well as foreign.

"Grief teaches the steadiest minds to waiver"

Sophocles

Historically, society exemplifies males as confident, in control, task oriented and capable of enduring physical and emotional pain. This image directly conflicts with their need to grieve the death of their spouse, which is perhaps why their propensity for instrumental grieving emerges.

Grief groups provide an important resource for men, since they often refrain from public grieving. "Many men who grieve never discuss their feelings regarding a loss."[47] They can especially benefit from grief groups attended by other males. It is often essential for widowers with children to connect with other widowers raising children.

I recall one man in particular whose wife died from cancer at the age of 37. He worked in a factory six days a week and had to leave home at 4:00 a.m. They had two young children and his wife had worked at home, in a super mom capacity. He now had some significant complications in addition to his grief. Where would he find a babysitter who could start work at 4:00 a.m. six days a week? It would be helpful if this babysitter could also cook, clean house, do laundry and pay bills.

The secondary losses resulting from the death of a wife also influence how the widower adjusts to his new life. Men seek new relationships for many reasons, including the necessity to fill gaps left by their wife's death, such as companionship and household tasks.

This experience is especially true with older males who are accustomed to traditional roles and thus are untrained in completing the tasks. I have watched men struggle with the necessity of taking on all of their wives' former functions and roles within the family. It is not easy to replace a super mom, who bakes, decorates, hosts dinner parties and makes matching Halloween costumes for the entire family.

In addition, men generally have fewer friends outside of their couple status and associate in fewer social circles and this can result in their seeking out the companionship that women traditionally find with their female friends. In America today there are very few organizations or gathering places catering only to men. As such, they seldom have the opportunity to socialize.

Men frequently start dating or seek companionship faster than their female counterparts do, because to a strong degree they experience the loss of their spouse as the loss of a companion, and a domestic and sexual partner.[48] Periodically, they rush this dating process and as a result, their new relationship falters or fails.

Commonly, adult children report feeling angry or frustrated that their fathers are dating so quickly and see this as a betrayal. If shortly after your spouse died, you engaged in a new relationship, it could benefit you to acknowledge your motives and not mistake or confuse your need for companionship and domestic assistance with love.

*"It's sad when our daddies die.
Makes us one less
person inside"*

Pamela Ribon, 2003

The Children and their Grief

If you harbor any doubts about the impact of a parental death on a young child, consider this story of an eighty-four year old woman whom I had the pleasure of meeting one day. As we began talking she instantly took me back to when she was four years old (1923) and attending the county fair with her grandparents. She wore a new pink and white flowered dress her mother had given her that morning and she talked about how she thought it was the best day of her life.

However, after they arrived home from the fair, they found her mother in the kitchen crying because her father had just died in a car accident. She said, "Our lives changed that day. Things were never the same. My mom was never truly happy again." Yet, on this day, in 2003, having never met her before, the only thing she wanted to talk about was that significant moment in her life, 80 years earlier.

Your predominant instinct as a parent is to protect your children, physically and emotionally. Unfortunately, when their other parent dies, there is very little you can do to make your children feel better. Their grief and the extent of their loss rip you apart and you are left feeling helpless. All you can do is hold them when they cry and strive to keep everything else as normal as possible.

Children have multiple stages of development. How you talk to them about this loss and how they comprehend what has happened, often depends on their stage of development at the time of the loss. However, they will move through these stages of development, experiencing a new awareness of the death at each level, long after the adults in their lives have reconciled their own losses. This proves challenging for all surviving parents. It is helpful if you can recognize these new stages of development, as they occur, in order to help your children navigate their newly awakened emotions. In essence, they will grieve at each stage however, how they grieve changes as they mature.

Keep in mind that this information applies in general, that exceptions always apply and that this list is not all-inclusive. There are numerous books available, which focus specifically on children's grief and many are worth reading. In reviewing this information, it is up to you to discern which stage or combination of stages apply to your child.

Before age three, children see the world in a magical way and thus they are incapable of grasping the permanency of anything. For them, this means that death is temporary. In their egocentricity, they are convinced that the world centers on them and thus they often view death as abandonment. They may express concern that the remaining adults in their lives will also abandon them.

Children age three to six still hold on to their belief in magic, however they can also now experience added emotions including fear and guilt. They may not grieve because they continue to believe that death is reversible and thus fail to comprehend the finality of the situation. However, they will likely realize that something has changed. If they believe that mom or dad is in heaven, they may suggest that someone go to heaven and bring them back or they may express a desire to be in both places at once.

It is important to listen to what they are saying, as they may believe that they are responsible for their parent's death. Occasionally, children regress and you note a return of bed-wetting or thumb sucking behaviors. Therapists call this regression and it stems from the child wanting to return to the age when everything was okay. Thus, since mom or dad was still alive when they were three they regress to their stage of development at age three, back to the time when it was okay to wet their beds or suck their thumbs.

Many children in this age range express their grief through art such as painting, drawing, sand play etc. Nick, at age four, repeatedly drew a picture of the interior of our house with everyone sleeping in single beds. In his drawing, he illustrated a monster sneaking in to the house and taking his daddy while he slept. It is always important to ask your child to explain the picture to you, as it may mean something different to them.

Children age six to twelve possess more concrete thoughts and feelings and want facts and honest answers. If you are unable to answer their questions, try asking them the same question in return and see what their answer is. Their purpose in asking these questions is often because they want to share with you what they think.

They may see their parent's death as personal or as a punishment and they want to know how the death will affect them personally. Will they have to move, or change schools? Will you re-marry? They seek reassurance that someone will meet their needs without further disruptions.

They may have problems at school, anger management issues, and occasionally suicidal ideations, which means that keeping an open line of communication is crucial. Mike and some of his friends engaged in funeral play after attending Joe's funeral. While this can be disconcerting for the surviving parent, it appeared to help them. Mike's best grief therapy came while playing basketball with his grief counselor, as it was more comfortable for him to talk while engaged in a sporting activity. In retrospect, he probably did not even realize he was in counseling at the time.

A child age twelve to eighteen focuses on the fact that they are different from other teens who have not experienced a parental death. At this age, they are capable of abstract thinking. Common emotions include depression, anger and non-compliance. Because communication and independence are vital at this stage of development, if they do not grieve at the time of the death, their emotions often erupt once they leave home for college or elsewhere.

With children of all ages, it is helpful to remember that the sense of vulnerability you may be feeling is even stronger for them. This is extremely difficult when children incur simultaneous losses. My friend Debbie's youngest child, Catherine, experienced the death of her father and uncle within a short time span. At the age of five, she sat on my lap one day and said, "I think I need a break from funerals for awhile. They make me really sad." With kids who have experienced multiple losses, it is imperative that you continue to give them honest information. Since they have had first hand experience with loss, they know if you or someone else is not being truthful with them.

If their parent died when they were young, their awareness and acknowledgement of the death will transform as they traverse the stages of development. When Nick was nine, we arrived at his school where I also happened to be working at the time and I said, "I won't be able to pick up that movie because I am not coming home after work" Mike replied, "Why not, are you going to die?" Though slightly shocked by his comment, I managed to say, "No, I just have to go to the hospital and work until later tonight" Nick got very quiet. However, twenty minutes later, he ran into my classroom and threw himself into my arms sobbing uncontrollably.

After much conversation and analysis, I discovered that for the first time in Nick's life, he realized that his father had walked out the door and had never come home. For months afterwards, he would make sure he hugged me goodbye and insisted on telling me that he loved me whenever I left the house. He told his stepfather, Chris, that he did this because he did not know whether I would die that day.

The following summer I took Nick to a kid's grief retreat. After the retreat, I asked him how it went, since he was five ½ years out from his dad's death, and I wasn't sure if he would benefit. After giving it some thought, he replied, "For the first time in my life, I realized that dad is never coming home," an awareness he was not capable of at age four.

One of the problems facing widowed parents is determining whether their child is actually experiencing a grief burst or just a normal emotional response to growing up. With my children, I tried to establish if there was a trigger, i.e. date of death, an approaching holiday or other significant date. It helps to remember that their grief can mirror yours so if something triggers your grief it will likely trigger theirs as well.

When talking to children about death it is important to be honest and brevity is acceptable, as they do not usually require a lengthy explanation. Explain the difference between being alive and being dead and never assume a child is too young to understand the various aspects of death. Nick was acutely aware of the sadness that had settled in our house, and of the absence of his father, even though he failed to grasp the permanency of the situation.

I caution people against using cliché's that will induce fear or anger that can result in sleepless nights. Some examples are *He just went to sleep and died; it was God's will; He is in a better place; He went to the hospital and died; Mommy left on a trip, and won't be back for a long time.* Remember that kids in general are literal in their comprehension.

A woman in a grief group stated that she had arranged for her 8-year-old son to stay with friends on the night his dad died. The next day when he returned home, they told him his dad had died in his sleep. As a result, her son did not want anyone in the house to go to sleep at night. She had to take him to a counselor who helped her explain that dad died because he had cancer, not because he went to sleep.

They also had to assure him that when in the future he spent the night at a friend's house, no one else in his own home was going to die. They talked about the circle of life and about how in nature everything that is born must die. In concluding her story, his mother said, "I would have preferred that his first experience with death had involved a gold fish."

Normal grief reactions in children mirror those in adults and include anger, fear, guilt, shock, denial, sadness, regression, and depression. Remember that children also grieve differently from each other. Mike's primary emotion was anger and Nick's was sadness. Often, the things I tried to help them through their grieving process worked for only one of them. After Joe died, I took them to his office to see if they wanted to take anything home. Mike found the experience helpful and even fun. Nick got a stomachache and wanted to go home.

Art Linkletter and subsequently Bill Cosby hosted a show entitled, "Kids Say the Darndest Things." This phenomenon is never more evident than when working with children in grief. Kids will want to talk when it is convenient for them, not for you, so keep yourself available for when they are ready. Share your feelings with your children, and if they do not like to see you cry let them know that sometimes you have no choice.

Mike and Nick did their best grief work when we were in the car. At four and seven, they still rode in the back seat. Maybe the contained area of the car provided an added sense of security or maybe they felt safe because they were talking to the back of my head. (If I started crying, they wouldn't have to watch). For whatever reasons their major league questions and gut wrenching statements came in route to or from, wherever we were going or had just been.

Cruising through town reminiscing about their day at school or at play and always unexpectedly came the difficult questions. Such as, *was there a lot of blood on dad's face? What was the last thing dad thought before he died? Did dad commit suicide? Did he die with his eyes open or closed? Did he pray before he died? Did Jeff and Brian do everything they could to save him?* After church one day, the boys wanted to know the significance of Joe not getting last rites before he died. Sometimes, they just wanted to know when the rest of their family was going to die.

A most memorable moment came after Nick and I visited the cemetery, when he was five. For a while on the ride home, he remained quiet. Then he said, "Mom, what does dad look like right now?" I sat stunned, thinking how to tell a five year old, what his dad might look like four months after burial. I looked to the sky in silent prayer, and then responded in the form of a question. I said, "What do you think he looks like?" He thought for a few moments and replied, "I think he looks like he is about five years old." I quit holding my breath and said, "Yeah, I think you're right."

I recall Joe's brother John driving us in New York one day, and Mike was in the back seat. I was telling John about the book I had read by Harold Kushner, *Why Bad Things Happen to Good People*. Mike spoke up from the back seat saying, "Why would you read that? Nothing bad happened to you, the bad thing happened to dad." It was difficult to argue with his logic.

The children and the staff at the boy's school were incredibly supportive of us, though some of the kids struggled with the fear of losing their own fathers. One day following a counseling session, Nick returned to school in time for lunch. He sat next to one of his schoolmates, who after asking where he had been, said, "My brother's dad died when he was two, you got to have your dad until you were four. Man you are really lucky!"

Unfortunately, anyone with children also knows about bullying behaviors, especially in middle school. Though Mike and Nick's experience with bullies pertaining to their father's death was limited, others are not so lucky. I have heard about several instances of middle school aged boys whose dad had died and their subsequent encounters with the school bullies. Statements such as, *Your dad died to get away from*

*you; You could have saved your dad, if you were any kind of a man; Now
that your dad is dead, I guess that makes you a bastard.*

If your kids suffered this type of behavior, make sure you contact
their schools. They should have an anti-bullying policy in place and they
need to know that this type of bullying occurs.

Working with your kids through their grief process is the most
important thing you can do following the death of your spouse. Never
assume that they are too young to understand; never think they cannot
handle the truth; never quit answering their questions and give them
every opportunity to heal. They usually will want to talk about their
deceased parent and it is crucial that you keep this line of communication open, especially if you have remarried.

> *Many adults whose parent died when they were young
> have expressed regret in the fact that their surviving parent
> did not talk about the death or about the deceased parent
> and in choosing this route disallowed or discouraged their
> children as well.*

I felt it was important and necessary to tell the boys that their father
did not intend to die. However, he did make some poor choices that
ultimately resulted in his death and by saying this; I discouraged their
placing the blame elsewhere. Father Seamus may have summed it up
best at Joe's funeral when he said that the difference between humans
and animals is that humans have freedom of choice and that sometimes
they make bad choices.

Five years after Joe's death, Nick wrote, "I honor my dad because
he was very kind and smart. I just wish he did not go snowmobiling on
January 31, 2001. My life would not have changed."

As a fifth grade English assignment, the students wrote a letter to
Santa Claus on behalf of their parents. Mike wrote:

> *"Dear Santa: My dad was very good throughout the
> years he was alive. I would really appreciate it if you would
> go up to Heaven and give him a Major League Baseball
> bat signed by the Yankees baseball team. If you want proof
> that he was a very good dad, I will tell you some things*

that he did well. He taught me how to play sports. He also taught me to be fair while playing sports and not to be a poor winner or a poor loser. He also taught me how to make pancakes. The last three things he taught me were to be smart, to build things, and to be nice to other people. As you can see, my dad deserves this baseball bat, so please bring it to him?"

When widowed with young children, it quickly dawns on you what it means to be the remaining biological parent. You alone will have to make all of the decisions, experience all of the joys, concerns, and complications. At first, this awareness is overwhelming, but after many missed celebrations, holidays, awards and milestones, you get accustomed to their absence and it can eventually seem less sad.

I still find that for the boys, we miss Joe the most in the best and the worst of times and on the first and last day of each school year. Spending Father's Day at the cemetery will probably always be troubling and I feel guilty celebrating this day with my dad, in the presence of my sons.

Immediately after Joe's death, I feared that I might also die soon or at least before my children reached adulthood. I started counting the years and months in between, in which staying alive was imperative. Then one day, many years later, I realized that they would survive without me too and that meant I could let go of my fear. In doing so, I was at least free to be present in their lives, today, if not tomorrow.

"The universe is made of stories, not of atoms."

Muriel Rukeyser

Funerals and Memorials

Every life is a compilation of stories and we have the opportunity to honor that life by telling their story. We can accomplish this in many ways through their funeral service as well as public and private memorials. How we do this can vary significantly depending on the age and manner in which our companion died. The funeral for an 80-year old war veteran looks and feels quite differently than one for a 40-year-old mother.

As the surviving spouse, we must make decisions about funeral and burial services as well as memorials, and often without a road map of any kind. Again, if we never discussed these issues with our spouse before he died we can only guess what he would have wanted or make choices based on what we feel is best.

For the past several decades in this country, churches and funeral homes supplanted the customs and rituals that historically took place in the privacy of the deceased's home. This new way, sterile and detached afforded us a safe distance from death. Many survivors chose closed casket or at least delayed viewing until the funeral. When my husband died, he sustained severe head and facial injuries and as a result, the funeral director discouraged viewing, though our priest strongly disagreed. In the end, I opted out, primarily because of my fear of what his injuries would look like and if they would prevent us from being able to recall his face, undamaged. In her writings and teachings, Elizabeth Kubler-Ross contended that seeing the body provides family members and friends with necessary closure.[49] I believe she was probably correct; however, I choose not to regret my decision.

Nick repeatedly questioned why I had not allowed him to see Joe's body, which ultimately became an issue that we dealt with in counseling. Fortunately, the counselor assured me that, had I opted for viewing, we would be talking about the effect from that decision in counseling. It was the proverbial no win situation.

Finding a meaningful way to memorialize your loved one can bring you and others great comfort. At the request of Joe's mom, I arranged for a memorial bench at a park overlooking the Puget Sound and adjacent to railroad tracks. I made "Dad and Me" books for each of the boys. For friends and family I selected the following poem by Canon Henry Scott-Holland and had it framed with a photo of Joe.

"Death is nothing at all
I have only slipped away into the next room
I am I and you are you
Whatever we were to each other
That we are still
Call me by my old familiar name
Speak to me in the easy way you always used
Put no difference into your tone,
Wear no forced air of solemnity or sorrow.
Laugh as we always laughed
At the little jokes we always enjoyed together
Play, smile, think of me, pray for me
Let my name be ever the household word that it always was
Let it be spoken without effort
Without the ghost of a shadow in it
Life means all that it ever meant
It is the same as it ever was
There is absolute unbroken continuity
What is death but a negligible accident?
Why should I be out of mind
Because I am out of sight?
I am waiting for you, for an interval
Somewhere very near.
Just around the corner.
All is well."

In truth, I often felt let down after completing something in Joe's memory. I believe these feelings stemmed from my hope that the project would accelerate my healing process and perhaps it did, but not quite quickly enough. In retrospect, I am thankful that I arranged for and created these memorials for Mike and Nick's sake, because they will get to know their father better through these and other tributes.

"We are not human beings
having a spiritual experience.
We are spiritual beings
having a human experience"

Pierre Teilhard de Chardin

Spirituality

The spiritual dilemmas that at times arise following the death of a spouse range from the "why" questions to expressing anger at God. Regardless of where you stand on the spiritual spectrum, this experience will likely reveal or allow you to discover your genuine perceptions of life, death and the afterlife.

At some juncture in your grieving process, you may search for the existential meaning of your relationship as well as for the lessons learned by having experienced the end of your physical relationship.

You may reach a point where you can focus on the enrichment gained in enduring this loss with the ultimate goal being the ability to say to your late spouse, *it was my privilege to have known you*, having no regrets for the relationship, just that it ended.

Many people have not examined their religious or spiritual beliefs, regardless of their church attendance record. Their parents took them to church every weekend and they continued that practice throughout their lives without giving much thought to what they actually believed. However, I believe that if the issue of death and dying does not perpetuate a spiritual exploration, then probably nothing will.

Having said that, there are people who possess an absolute faith, who have reached a level of comfort and understanding in their belief system. In situations such as these, death and dying does not necessarily bring about a new examination or a shift in faith.

Distinguishing between spirituality and religion is important because of the chasm that currently exists between them. It is interesting to note that at some point in our country, these terms became contrary. Today people often further this separation by emphasizing that they are *spiritual but not religious.*

M.C. Gilbert defines religion as, "The visible expressions of beliefs through liturgies, rituals, symbols, doctrines, and creeds that serves to identify persons and groups as members of a particular denomination."[50] In summation, religion is the formal expression of our relationship with the transcendent.

Mr. Gilbert defines spirituality as a "Human quest for personal meaning and mutually fulfilling relationships among people, the non-human environment, and, for some, God."[51] In essence, relationships are the foundation of spirituality and this can include a relationship with God. The realm of spirituality encompasses hope, faith, meaning, purpose and love.

In having survived something as significant as the death of your spouse, you also probably experienced some measure of spiritual or religious exploration and the results of this review may have surprised you. "Finding meaning begins in questioning. Those who do not search do not find."[52] In essence, no one truly understands their beliefs until they have examined them in depth, and this momentous alteration of your life affords you this opportunity.

Your own cultural and religious beliefs can influence your grief and your reconciliation of that grief. People who believe in God and Heaven and believe that their spouse is with God in Heaven often express surprise at the level of grief they experience after their spouse has died. Some people do not find solace in their faith. I believe C.S. Lewis said it best in his book *A Grief Observed*, "Talk to me about the truth of religion and I'll listen gladly. Talk to me about the duty of religion and I'll listen submissively. But don't come talking to me about the consolations of religion or I shall suspect that you don't understand."[53]

If in the past you had no reason or desire to explore spiritual issues, then experiencing death first or second hand frequently galvanizes this desire. Investing time and energy in examining your belief systems, your assessment of the life you have lived or are living, and your interpretation of the meaning you ascribe to this life can help you assimilate the path your life has now taken. Thus, regardless of your beliefs in an after-life, spirituality by definition encompasses the meaning you ascribe to this life.

It is important to recognize that spiritual questions and trepidation exist for non-religious or non-spiritual people as well. Even professed agnostics and atheists explore and question the meaning and purpose of life when facing imminent death. "Over 50 percent of people without previous religious involvement said they wanted to discuss spiritual issues." [55]

In researching this issue, I found this poem, which I felt was ironically humorous.

"Like pond-bound fish under global vaults of air,
Speckled by beams from up beyond our sight,
Whence luster menaces yet entices,
What shall we make of the light?" [54]

If you had moments with your dying spouse to talk about his beliefs, concerns and fears then you witnessed a desire that we have to share our thoughts on the meaning we ascribe to our life and impending death. Many times, we are speaking these thoughts for the first and possibly the only time, thus careful listening at this time is imperative. Ram Dass said, "All I can really do is create a spacious environment within my own mind that allows someone else to die as he or she needs to die." The best any of us can do when in the presence of a dying person is to provide them an audience.

Therefore, it is crucial that as the listener we set aside our own beliefs, avoiding indifference or reluctance in order to fully share in this moment.[56] Nursing home, hospital and hospice workers must ascribe similar sensitivity and awareness when they address spiritual and religious diversity as utilized when addressing the more commonly recognized diversities.[57]

Frequently, dying people question why the actual process is taking so long. They have accepted their prognosis and are now prepared to die, which makes it difficult for them to understand why they are still alive. As a possible explanation, there are those who believe that dying engages us in spiritual growth and therefore those who encounter us at this time are able to experience growth at an accelerated rate. Therefore, the dying while engaged in dying, are also teaching and promoting spiritual growth for those of us around them.

A frequently voiced concern of patients is that they do not want to be a burden for families. Unfortunately, most individuals consider any help from others burdensome. Thus, when family and friends want to help them, they equate accepting the offer with being a burden. The key is to help your dying spouse understand that accepting assistance is as beneficial to him as it is to us because in addition to our wanting to help, helping affords us spiritual growth.

The following reading provides comfort for those who believe in an after-life. However, it is important to understand that believing may diminish but does not eradicate your grief. Even if you believe that your spouse lives eternally, he is not here for you to touch, to talk to or to hold. It is comforting, though not easy, if you can transform your relationship from what it was before to what it is now, while simultaneously acknowledging your loss:

To Those Who Mourn, by C.W. Leadbeater

For that is the real truth;
Man is a soul and has a body.
The body is not the man;
It is only the clothing of the man.
What you call death is the laying aside
Of a worn-out garment,
And it is no more the end of the man
Than it is the end of you
When you remove your coat.
Therefore, you have not lost your friend;
You have only lost sight of the cloak
In which you were accustomed to see him.
The cloak is gone.
But the man who wore it is not;
Surely it is the man that you love
And not the garment.

People have interesting opinions and beliefs around what they might call karma or God's will. A very well meaning friend from church assured me within days of my husband' funeral, that since we had experienced this terrible loss, nothing else bad would happen to us. Since I did not feel particularly insulated from bad things at that moment, I felt it best not to respond.

I believe that life consists of hills and valleys and we cannot truly appreciate the good times without having experienced the bad times. We all know of people who have endured multiple losses and if you live long enough, you will do so at the expense of having outlived many, if not all, of your family members and friends.

> *Life expectancy dictates that as we age, the likelihood of our imminent death increases. Unfortunately, when someone dies out of the natural order, a younger person, or children before parents, it does not prevent the natural deaths from occurring, nor does one tragedy preclude other traumatic events.*

We have heard the old and at times overused adage; *it must have been his time to die.* In analyzing that statement, you realize that this is a palindrome of sort. He died because it was his time, or in reverse, it must have been his time, because he died. In essence, the event supports the theory and the theory supports the event.

My personal beliefs, (which no one has to agree with) include a combination of randomness, a master plan and spiritual evolution. I also believe that with this plan our time of death is predestined at the time of our birth. This belief helps me cope with my own loss as well as the deaths of the people I meet in hospice work, people of all ages who are at varied levels of achievement and enlightenment, without wondering why them or why now.

I have shared this theory with friends on occasion and some respond that if my theory is true, then the choices we make in life are meaningless. (If our predestined time to die is 80, smoking, or excessive eating will not result in an earlier death) However, keep in mind that our choices are vital to the type of life we live. (You may live to age 80, but because you smoked and over indulged, your quality of life is poor due to bad health) In essence, it is not about how long we live, but about how well we live, which is a direct outcome of our choices, and occasionally other people's choices.

Obviously, we cannot know why, when or how we will die, nor can we know with absolute certainty exactly what happens after death. However, I find comfort in believing in the time to die theory as well as in believing that our souls transcend this life. Having held these beliefs is unlikely to cause me or anyone else harm, if at the time of my death, I find out that I am wrong.

In hospice work, when we ask people about their faith affiliation, they often avoid responding altogether or they may respond by stating which church they attend or simply state that they are "Christian" without any further discussion. Many people choose not to discuss their beliefs, some because they may not really know what they want to say and many because they are wary of forthcoming judgment.

This wariness is valid because often instead of applauding individualism, many people judge those who do not believe as they do. What would the world be like today if we all embraced the notion that we do not have to hold the same beliefs, that being different is acceptable, that there may be more than one acceptable answer?

Religious and spiritual beliefs are significantly personal, molded by a lifetime of events as well as assimilation of information and development of individual perceptions. It makes sense that the individualization of this process negates any possibility of a universal belief system and supports the belief that there exist as many differences within each religious framework as there are between the various religions.

The spiritual perspective is germane, though not mandatory, to the philosophy of hospice, palliative and end-of-life care. I am hopeful that with the rapid aging of American society, coupled with the resurgence of acknowledging death and dying, we will invest more time examining our belief systems.

"Laughter catches in our throat because we refuse to accept the corollary of joy, the soul-enriching poignancy of loss."

David Whyte

Life Goes On: Signs of Healing

In the six years following Joe's death, we moved twice, I finished graduate school, changed careers, re-married and wrote this book. Nick at age eleven is an established violin player in the Tacoma Youth Symphony. Mike, who is now fourteen, excels in athletics, especially baseball. If someone had described my current life six years earlier, I would not have believed in or recognized that life.

Everything changed because of a single choice someone else made. No one who has experienced the death of a spouse stays the same, even if these changes are not apparent to others. The experience of the death, the loss and the subsequent grief influences every aspect of your life. Perhaps we made some mistakes, some incorrect choices along the way. The key is that we survived.

Eventually, time eases the shock and pain. However, the event will always remain in your mind, heart and soul. "Mourning never really ends. Only as time goes on, it erupts less frequently."[58] I have read countless books, brochures, poems and stories. This meditative poem is my favorite and thus a fitting way to conclude this book.

It is written by Rabbi Harold M. Schulweis, Valley Beth Shalom (Encino, California). He is the founder of the Jewish Foundation for the Righteous and the author of *For Those Who Can't Believe*.

Playing with Three Strings

We have seen Yitzhak Perlman
Who walks the stage with braces on both legs,
On two crutches.

He takes his seat, unhinges the clasps of his legs,
Tucking one leg back, extending the other,
Laying down his crutches, placing the violin under his chin.

On one occasion one of his violin strings broke.
The audience grew silent but the violinist did not leave the stage.
He signaled the maestro, and the orchestra began its part.
The violinist played with power and intensity on only three
    strings.

With three strings, he modulated, changed and
Recomposed the piece in his head
He retuned the strings to get different sounds,
Turned them upward and downward.

The audience screamed delight,
Applauded their appreciation.
Asked later how he had accomplished this feat,
The violinist answered
It is my task to make music with what remains.

A legacy mightier than a concert.
Make music with what remains.
Complete the song left for us to sing,
Transcend the loss,
Play it out with heart, soul, and might
With all remaining strength within us.

I think you will probably know when your grief diminishes enough that you can once again enjoy life's pleasantries. Bedtime no longer represents bad time. You will look backwards and forwards without sorrow and dread. You will create your new normal and recognize your new life patterns as yours. You will know that your recovery is not only possible but also happening right before your own eyes. It is now your time to make music with what remains.

End Notes

1.   Canine, 1996

2.   Bonnano et al, 2002

3.   Baird & Rosenbaum, 2003

4.   Welshons, J. E. 2000, p. 60

5.   Morrison, R. S. & Meier, D. E. 2004, p. 2582

6.   Luptak, 2004

7.   Graham, J, 2006

8.   Brant, 1998, p. 1000

9.   Welshons, 2000, p. 61

10.   Brant, 1998

11.   N. Mullen, personal communication, November 2002

12.   Morrison & Morris, 1995, p. 45

13.   Morrison et al, 2004, p. 2582

14.   Barriers, 2000, p. 83

15.   Lamont, 2004, p. 19

16.   Barriers, 2000, & Lamont, 2004

17.   Lamont, 2004, p. 19

18.   D. Hamill, personal communication, December 6, 2006

[19]   Lamont, 2004, p. 19

[20]   USDHHS, 2004

[21]   Quality of life matters, 2006, volume 8, issue 2, p. 1

[22]   Hobart, 2001, p. 191

[23]   NHPCO, 2004a

[24]   NHPCO, 2004 (c)

[25]   James & Gilliland, 2001

[26]   Kubler-Ross, 1974

[27]   Longaker, C. 1997, p. 198

[28]   Kenyon, 2001, p. 65

[29]   Colgrove, Bloomfield & McWilliams, 1991, p. 21

[30]   M. Ogilivie, personal communication, October 21, 2004

[31]   Strange, 2002, p. 147

[32]   McNeil, 1995, p. 288

[33]   Author unknown

[34]   Colgrove, et al, p. 23

[35]   Wolfelt, A., 2003, p. 75

[36]   Doss, 2002

[37]   Neimeyer, et al, 2002

[38]   Neimeyer et al, 2002

[39]   Neimeyer et al, 2002

[40]   Neimeyer et al, 2002, p. 239

[41]   Welshons, 2000, p. 187

[42]   Sanders, 1999, p. 262-263

[43]   Klass, 1999, p. 171

[44] Klass, 1999

[45] Neimeyer et al., 2002

[46] Kemp, 1997

[47] Staudacher, 1991, P. 16

[48] Staudacher, 1991

[49] Kubler-Ross, 1969

[50] Gilbert, 2000, p. 68

[51] Gilbert, 2000, p. 68

[52] Wolfelt, 2003, p. 156

[53] Lewis, C.S., 1961, p. 28

[54] Author Unknown

[55] Smith, D. C., 1997, p. 151

[56] Conrad, 1999

[57] Canda, 1997

[58] Wolfelt, A. 2003, p. 145

References

Baird, R. M., & Rosenbaum, S. E. (2003). Introduction. In R. M. Baird, & S. E. Rosenbaum (Eds.), *Caring for the dying: Critical issues at the end of life* (pp. 9– 24). Amhurst, N.Y: Prometheus Books. *Barriers to hospice care: Are we shortchanging dying patients: Hearings before the Special Committee on Aging of the Senate,* 106th Cong., 83 (2000a) (testimony of Kathryn Grigsby).

Bonanno, G. A., Wortman, C. B., Lehman, D. R., Tweed, R. G., Haring, M., Sonnega, J. et al. (2002). *Journal of Personality and Social Psychology,* 83(5), 1150-1164.

Brant, J. M. (1998). The art of palliative care: Living with hope, dying with dignity. *Oncology Nursing Society,* 25(6), 995-1003.

Canine, J. D. (1996). *The psychosocial aspects of death and dying.* Stamford, CN: Appleton& Lange.

Canda, E. R. (1997). Spirituality. In R. L. Edwards (Ed.), *Encyclopedia of social work 19th edition, 1997 supplement* (pp. 299-306). Washington D.C: NASW Press.

Chapple, H. S. (2003). Changing the game in the intensive care unit letting nature take its course. In R. M.Baird, & S. E. Rosenbaum (Eds.), *Caring for the dying: Critical issues at the end of life* (pp. 47-71). Amhurst, N.Y: Prometheus Books.

Chochinov, H. M., (2004a). *Interventions to enhance the spiritual aspects of dying. NIH State-of-the-science conference on improving end-of-life care.* Retrieved January 18, 2005 from http://www.consensus.hih. gov

Chochinov, H. M., Hassard, T., & Janson, J. K. (2004). Dignity and psychotherapeutic considerations in end-of-life care. *Journal of Palliative Care, 20*(3), 134-142.

Colgrove, M., Bloomfield, H. H., & McWilliams, P. (1991). *How to survive the loss of a love.* Los Angeles, CA: Prelude Press.

Conrad, A. P. (1991). Critique: Professional tools for religiously and spirituallysensitive social work practice. In R. R. Green (Ed.), *Human behavior theory and social work practice* (2nd Ed.) (pp 63-71). New York: Aldine DeGruyter.

Doss, E. (2002). Death, art and memory in the public sphere: The visual and material culture of grief in contemporary America. *Mortality, 7*(1), 63-82.

Gilbert, M. C. (2000). Spirituality in social work groups: Practitioners speak out. *Social Work with Groups, 22*(4), 67-84.

Graham, J. Studies urge talk about final wishes. (2006, September 14). The News Tribune, p. A1.

Hobart, K. R. (2001). Death and dying and the social work role. *Journal of Gerontological Social Work, 36*(3/4), 181-192.

James, R. K., & Gilliland, B. E. (2001). *Crisis intervention strategies.* Belmont, CA: Wadsworth/Thomson Learning.

Kemp, S. P., Whittaker, J. K., & Tracy, E. M. (1997). *Person-environment practice: The social ecology of interpersonal helping.* New York: Aldine De Gruyter.

Kenyon, B. L. (2001). Current research in children's conceptions of death: A critical review.*OMEGA, 43*(1), 63-91.

Klass, D. (1999). Developing a cross-cultural model of grief: The state of the field. *OMEGA, 39*(3), 153-178.

Koenig, H. G. (2002). A commentary: The role of religions and spirituality at the end of life. *The Gerontologist, 42*, Special Issue III, 20-23.

Kubler-Ross, E. (1969). *On death and dying.* N.Y: Simon & Schuster.

Kubler-Ross, E. (1974) *Questions and answers on death and dying.* N.Y: Macmillan Publishing.

Lamont, E. (2004). A demographic and prognostic approach to defining the end of life. *NIH State-of-the-science conference on improving end-of-life care.* Retrieved January 18, 2005 from http://www.consensus.hih.gov

Lewis, C. S. (1961). *A grief observed.* N.Y: Seabury Press Inc.

Longaker, C. 1997. *Facing death and finding hope.* N.Y: Broadway Books.

Luptak, M. (2004). Social work and end-of-life care for older people: A historical perspective. *Health & Social Work,* 29(1), 7-15.

McNeil, J. S. (1995). Bereavement and loss. In L. Beebe (Ed.), *Encyclopedia of social work 19th edition* (pp. 284-290). Washington D.C: NASW Press.

Morrison, R. S. & Meier, D. E. (2004). *Palliative care,* 2582-2590. Retrieved June 21, 2004 from https://www.nejm.org

Morrison, R. S. & Morris, J. (1995). When there is no cure: Palliative care for the dying patient. *Geriatrics, 50*(7), 45-51).

National Association of Social Workers. (2004, February). Palliative and end of life care highlights. In *Notes from the field...palliative and end of life care: Program, policy and practice.* Retrieved May 2, 2004, from http://www.socialworkers.org/practice/bereavement/021304notes.asp

National Hospice and Palliative Care Organization. (2004a). *Characteristics of U.S. hospice programs.* Retrieved October 24, 2004, from http://www.nhpco.org

National Hospice and Palliative Care Organization. (2004c). *Hospice & palliative care: History of hospice care.* Retrieved November 21, 2004, from http://www.nhpco.org

Neimeyer, R. A., Prigerson, H. G., & Davies, B. (2002). Mourning and meaning. *American Behavioral Scientist, 46*(2), 235-251.

Quality of life matters, Vol. 8, Issue 1 May/June/July 2006. Naples, Fl: Quality of Life Publishing Co.

Quality of life matters, Vol. 8, Issue 2 Aug/Sept/Oct 2006. Naples, Fl: Quality of Life Publishing Co.

Sanders, C. M. (1999). *Grief the mourning after: Dealing with adult bereavement* (2nd ed.). New York: John Wiley & Sons.

Saleebey, D. (2001). *Human behavior and social environments: A biopsychosocial approach.* New York: Columbia University Press

Smith, D. C. (1997). *Caregiving: Hospice-proven techniques for healing body and soul.* N.Y.: Wiley Publishing Co.

Speck, P. (2003). Spiritual/religious issues in care of the dying. In J. Ellershaw & S. Wilkinson (Eds.), Care of the dying: A pathway to excellence (pp. 90-105). NY: Oxford University Press.

Strange, J.M. (2002). She cried a very little: Death, grief and mourning in working-class culture. *Social History, 27*(2).

Staudacher, C. (1991). *Men & Grief.* Oakland, CA: New Harbinger Publications, Inc.

U.S. Census Bureau. (2000). Retrieved May 8, 2003, from http://www.census.gov

U.S. Census Bureau. (2002). Retrieved October 24, 2004, from http://www.census.gov/prod/2003pubs/02statab/pop.pdf

U.S. Department of Health and Human Services. [USDHHS] (2004, December). NIH panel issues state-of-the science statement on end-of-life care. *In NIH news– National Institutes of Health.* Retrieved January 18, 2005, from http://www.nih.gov/news/pr/dec2004 od-08.htm

Welshons, J. E. (2000). *Awaking from grief: Finding the road back to joy.* Little Falls, N.J: Open Heart Publications.

Wolfelt, A. D. (2003). *Understanding your grief.* Fort Collins, CO: Companion Press.

Made in the USA
Lexington, KY
23 April 2011